THE POLITICS OF REFORM

The Politics of Reform

PAR: 50 Years of Changing Louisiana

JOHN MAGINNIS

Public Affairs Research Council
Baton Rouge, Louisiana

Copyright © 2000 by the Public Affairs Research Council
All rights reserved
Published in the United States of America
First printing

ISBN: 0-9667795-1-7

Copy editing by Catherine L. Kadair
Editorial consulting by J. F. Cado
Page design and production by Melanie O'Quinn Samaha
Cover design by Stan Taylor, Gold Dust Graphics

ACKNOWLEDGMENTS

The *Baton Rouge Advocate* provided access to its newspaper files. The *Advocate* also loaned news photos from its files for use in this book. The *New Orleans Times-Picayune* granted permission to use editorial cartoons done by the late John Chase for the *States-Item*. Special recognition to the late John Wilds, whose book on the 30th anniversary of PAR proved to be a valuable resource.

Special thanks and appreciation to:
Freeport-McMoRan, Inc.
Jay Handelman
Louisiana Association of Broadcasters
Louisiana Press Association
Shell Exploration & Production Company
for underwriting this publication.

In memory of Pam Samaha

CONTENTS

Letter to the Citizens of Louisiana ix

1
The New Observer 1

2
Against the Tide 32

3
Meet the Master 61

4
Reckoning for Reform 85

5
One for History 109

Presidents/Chairmen of PAR 131

Dear Citizens of Louisiana:

This new century gives the Public Affairs Research Council the opportunity to focus on its future as well as to reflect upon its past. PAR celebrates its 50th anniversary in 2000—and what an interesting half century it's been for our organization. Granted, the word *interesting* is an understatement. After all, PAR has led the way in pressing for governmental reforms and, thus, has become at times a favorite punching bag for elected officials.

Overcoming many difficulties and challenges, PAR today is stronger than ever as it continues its role of making state government more responsive to the people, more efficient in its operations, more open in its decision making and more intelligent in its use of tax dollars.

All of this is brilliantly reflected in the 50th anniversary book on PAR by renowned political writer, commentator and historian John Maginnis. The PAR Executive Committee commissioned Maginnis to write a comprehensive history of the organization and gave him complete editorial freedom to tell the whole story of PAR, its good decisions and bad ones, its successes and failures.

The result is a masterfully written book that intertwines the history of state government since 1950—including its most controversial issues and fascinating politicians—and PAR's involvement in bringing about changes. We say thank you to John Maginnis for a job well done.

Finally, we want to give special recognition to the long list of staff members and volunteer leaders who have guided PAR through five decades. The founding members and staffers undertook the daunting task of forming a statewide organization to challenge the prevailing view that government was by and for the politicians and power brokers who tightly controlled it. As chronicled in this book, their task was far from easy, as they devoted time and resources far beyond what was expected of them. The many women and men who followed have been equally diligent and unselfish in furthering the mission of PAR. They all are civic heroes in the truest sense and deserve our eternal thanks.

Beginning our sixth decade, we can assure the people of Louisiana that PAR will continue its role of "government watchdog" with unbiased and vigorous research and reports. We've accomplished a great deal, but there is so much more to do. We will work hard—and we're certain we speak for those who will follow us—to make the next 50 years equally productive on behalf of you, the citizens of Louisiana.

Sincerely,

Jay Handelman
Chairman

James C. Brandt
President

THE POLITICS OF REFORM

1

THE NEW OBSERVER

Within hours of the governor calling a special session, to convene that evening, legislators were drifting into the bar of the Heidelberg Hotel in downtown Baton Rouge for a cocktail or two before heading over to the House chamber to hear what Earl Long wanted them to do. They had a pretty good idea.

Newspaper editorials in June 1951 huffed their usual complaint that there was no extraordinary need for the Legislature to gather outside of its biennial session—no invasions, natural disasters or massive fiscal shortfall, as the 1921 constitution had envisioned. Yet an "extraordinary session" of the Legislature had been scheduled quite regularly, every other year between ordinary sessions, for 30 years.

As usual for a special session, the real problem was not too little money, but too much. The state treasury was running a large surplus from new taxes and the surprising huge royalties and bonuses being paid by oil companies rushing to exploit the new offshore drilling technology. Earl Long intended to spend that money, lest it fall into the hands of the next governor.

"Governor Long realizes he can't name his successor, so he's intent on seeing the cupboard is bare before he leaves office," scowled Lt. Gov. Bill Dodd, who had recently been informed that he would not be Long's candidate in that year's election.

If any lawmakers were to complain that the session was unnecessary, Governor Long at least did not keep them working for long. He mainly needed their rubber-stamp to transfer $14 million to the Highway Department, whose director refused to tell the legislative committees what he would do with the money. Long also wanted to establish the state School for Spastic Children ("Are you against the spastics?" he challenged legislators in his opening address) and to take care of a few local favors, such as establishing a cemetery board for a ward in Morehouse Parish. The 32 bills drafted by administration floorleaders sailed through both chambers with barely a dissenting vote. In five days, the legislators' work was done and they went home, only to return ten days later to officially adjourn.

The only speed bump along the way was laid down by Lt. Gov. Dodd, the Senate presiding officer, who led a small rebellion on the first night of the session by ousting Long men from committee chairmanships and naming his own. It took Long only three days to crush the uprising and reinstall his chairmen, just in time for the Senate to adopt the bills sent over by the House.

In all, it was a fairly ordinary extraordinary session, routinely covered by the state's major newspapers and barely noticed even by the political class, which was already gearing toward the next governor's election.

Yet what made this special session historic was not the players but the observers. Passing unnoticed in the galleries and halls was a small band of researchers who tracked all bills, even read them, recorded all votes and developed the most complete—and damning—record of any meeting of the Legislature.

Still struggling to build its membership and to finance the small staff's operations from a cramped office in downtown Baton Rouge, the Public Affairs Research Council had entered the political arena it would profoundly change.

That would take some time.

Its 16-page report on that special session, published a month later, hardly rocked the foundation of the state's power structure. Yet it laid out in fine, almost comic, detail the executive domination of the legislative branch of government that was equal in name only. It noted how little time each bill was debated, if at all. Often, the author of a bill had not completed reading its title before the question was called.

Making its point graphically, the report ran a time line of the session over the bottom quarter of each page, noting what was done on each day, with a flat line running through the ten days the Legislature went home after rushing through the governor's package.

The slim volume was not widely circulated but it was read in the right places, from which its message spread.

The *New Orleans States-Item* commented, "We have always felt that special sessions of the state Legislature were operated on a hush-hush, wham-bam basis . . . an impressive statistical study by PAR confirms that belief."

Earl Long's reaction was not recorded, but it's a safe bet the governor was hardly bothered that the *Item* had found someone who agreed with it. At the end of his first full term in office, at the apex of his power, Earl Long was on his way toward eclipsing the achievements of his older brother Huey.

The colorful legend of Uncle Earl was mostly painted in his second and last full term, 1956–60, in which television news cameras and writers like A. J. Liebling chronicled his more outrageous rantings to the Legislature, his frolics with stripper girlfriend Blaze Starr, his trips to and from mental institutions. Yet Long's greatest impact on the state was felt in 1948–52, when he roared back into office, dismantled reforms passed in the previous administration and reinstated with ruthless efficiency his brand of strongman populist politics. Many of the new programs enacted, financed by increased taxes on businesses and consumers, indeed would help the poor and address social inequities. But Long would also add to the already high level of waste and corruption in state government.

The return of Earl Long stunned members of the leading business and professional class, who thought they had buried Longism a decade before.

A ruling class once ran Louisiana not from elected office but from boardrooms and back rooms in New Orleans and on plantations on the river. The so-called Bourbon elite (the name given the upper class who wrested back Louisiana government after Reconstruction, much like the French nobility restored to power after Napoleon) controlled politics in alliance with the ruling cabal of New Orleans politicians called the Old Regulars.

Governors tended to do the bidding of these powerful men, never more so than during the great flood of 1927, when a group of New Orleans bankers, attorneys and businessmen pressured Gov. O. H. Simpson to order the dynamiting of the levee in St. Bernard Parish in order to save the city. As documented in *Rising Tide* by John Barry, the act, later proved to be unnecessary, washed away the homes and farms of thousands of powerless residents downriver and stirred great resentment toward the power elite and the city of New Orleans. That resentment added to the wave of votes that swept the populist Huey Long into the governor's office in 1928. He broke the wealthy elite's grip of power over the state by taking it for himself.

Long spent heavily on roads, schools, hospitals and pensions, which helped the backward state begin to catch up from years of neglect under the reactionary Planter-Ring oligarchy. Yet in his drive for absolute power Long broached no dissent and made good on promises to crush those in his way. Business and political leaders in New Orleans found themselves unable to stop Long's program to vitiate the municipal powers of the city, thus extending his control to every corner of the state.

As often happens when rulers grow so powerful that change cannot come from within, it came instead from the barrel of a gun. After Long's assassination, federal prosecutors finished off his organization with a wave of criminal convictions, including Gov. Richard Leche and LSU President James Monroe Smith. Populism appeared to die at the ballot box when Earl Long, the lieutenant governor who succeeded Leche, lost the 1940 election to reformer Sam Jones.

The business interests, particularly in New Orleans, who had despaired during the Long years were heartened by the rapid pace of Jones's reforms, especially the establishment of civil service. The classified personnel system protected most state workers from wholesale quadrennial firings when a new governor took office and doled out jobs to supporters.

World War II and the business-friendly caretaker administration of Gov. Jimmie Davis, who did not let his executive duties interfere with his Hollywood career. The singing governor lulled conservatives into believing reform had taken root in Louisiana.

In a sense, Louisiana had been shamed into reform, but the people did not embrace it readily or for long. "There was a latent hostility toward the whole reform movement," recalled Joe D. Smith, then the business manager of the *Alexandria Daily Town Talk,* who would later become its publisher. "People had gotten a little shaken up by it. The whole change was too much."

So was the prospect of a second Sam Jones administration. The campaign of 1948 would be a rematch of the 1940 election, which Jones narrowly won, but Earl K. Long was not the same politician that Jones turned out of office eight years before.

Emerging from Huey's shadow, the 53-year-old Long was a more mature and self-assured candidate but remained every bit the flamboyant, charismatic crowd-pleaser. In courthouse squares and from the backs of flatbed trucks, Long regaled crowds with his stories and promises of active government. He dealt with opponents more deftly than did his brother, preferring ridicule to scorn, especially in the nicknames he gave them. Former governor Jones became "Sweet Smellin' Sam," and it stuck.

Recalling his own handicap eight years earlier of having to "run on another man's record," Long crowed, "Now Sam Jones must run on the record of eight years of do-nothing government during the Jones-Davis administration."

Jones tried to exploit Long's war record, calling him a "yellow slacker" for avoiding the draft until three weeks before the Armistice in 1918. Long returned fire: "Old Sam Jones didn't smell any powder. He never got farther than Camp Beauregard and his mama had to bring him cake every weekend to keep him there."

When Jones's car skidded on an icy road into a truck shortly before the first primary, Long expressed his concern: "I quit the campaign to go up there and see they doctored to him, 'cause I know if he died, they might put a good man in there that'd beat us both."

Jones survived the crash but not the election. Long led him 41–23 percent in the first Democratic primary before winning his first full term with 66 percent in the runoff.

To the dismay of business and professional leaders in the cities who thought they had buried Longism, it was back with a vengeance.

Setting a compliant Legislature through its paces, the new governor hit business and consumers alike with higher taxes on oil and gas, retail sales, gasoline, beer and cigarettes in order to pay for increased old-age pensions, free school lunches, free school-bus transportation, more state hospitals and more state employees. His state employees. The very hallmark of the reform years, the state civil service system, was scrapped so that Long could fill state jobs, from elevator operators to engineers, with legions of political supporters.

The increased government spending did correct many long-standing injustices. Long built two new charity hospitals and more than doubled the number of trade schools, all of which were needed. The school he demanded for "the spastics" is now the

Louisiana Special Education Center in Alexandria, still the only facility in the public school system that teaches developmentally disabled youth.

Long also addressed a blatant inequity in public education by equalizing pay for white and black teachers with the same years of service.

And though a free spender by that day's standard, Earl Long was no borrower. Apart from one bond issue for war veterans' bonuses, Long in three terms did not increase state debt by one dollar.

Earl Long's first full administration turned the promises of populism into unprecedented social progress. But at a cost. There were flocks of cronies on state payrolls, and there was little accounting for the millions spent by agencies like the Highway Department. The governor dispensed massive patronage by granting insurance policy commissions on state property, by appointing lawyers to help collect inheritance taxes, and by depositing hundreds of millions of dollars in banks that paid the state no interest. Much of that money found its way back to the governor and his friends through campaign contributions or direct payoffs.

Far more troubling was the governor's association with gangsters. In their book *The Saga of Earl Long and Louisiana Politics,* authors Michael Kurtz and Morgan Peoples cite a 1948 FBI field office report stating that Long received money from Carlos Marcello and his syndicate, who in return operated wide-open casinos in Jefferson and St. Bernard parishes and organized a prostitution ring in French Quarter bars.

Those who crossed the new governor learned he could be as vindictive as his older brother. Long's special target was New Orleans Mayor Chep Morrison, who had campaigned for Sam Jones against Long in 1940 and 1948. Picking up where Huey Long left off in the campaign against New Orleans, Earl Long prevailed upon the Legislature to pass constitutional amendments to cut the city's sales tax in half and to transfer much of the mayor's authority to a city council gerrymandered to give control to Long's allies, the Old Regulars.

Outside New Orleans, one grievance stood above all for advocates of reform. "One thing that did it for everybody was [the repeal of] civil service," said Joe Smith. "That was the trigger. . . . People knew if he succeeded, we could really be in for a long continuation of that kind of government."

Not all members of the Legislature condoned the governor's power grab, but they could not stop it. Besides the absence of a two-party system and an effective public interest lobby, the key to Earl Long's massive power over legislators was information, that which he had and they did not. This was especially true in state finance, which was layered with dozens of accounts and special funds, with varying fractions of different taxes dedicated to support each. The byzantine confection made it nearly impossible for the Legislature, the press or any outside group to know how much the state had or needed. Inexact biennial budgets produced surpluses that would be reappropriated in the regularly scheduled special sessions.

There was no way of telling, complained a newspaper editorial, if the $14 million highway appropriation of the 1951 special session "would bring more roads or more department." In one committee hearing, the head of the Highway Department smilingly ignored legislators who demanded a simple accounting of the highway fund. State departments were audited by an official appointed by the governor. He rarely found anything amiss.

The business lobby that existed was grossly ineffective at dealing with anything broader than their own special interests. The oil companies and some trade organizations, such as Associated General Contractors, focused on their specific agendas. The Louisiana Manufacturers' Association and the State Chamber of Commerce never got up the steam to advance a statewide issue or to stop a new administration tax proposal.

Beyond the scattered business associations, there was no one group, even an ineffective one, to speak for citizens who simply wanted clean and efficient state government for all its people.

Starting such an organization would not be easy.

Few were more dismayed at the return to power of Earl K. Long in 1948 than Edgar B. Stern of New Orleans. The wealthy investment broker and developer had been a preeminent though behind-the-scenes force in city and state affairs since the 1920s, following his marriage to Edith Rosenwald, the heir to a principal in Sears Roebuck.

The couple were leading philanthropists but also major agents of social progress, as they embraced causes far more liberal than their social and civic peers. Major donors to the United Negro College Fund, they helped found Dillard University in New Orleans and later endowed it with $2 million.

Stern was a visionary businessman who put Louisiana's first television station on the air. Edgar and Edith gave the license for WDSU-TV to their son Edgar Jr. as a wedding present in 1948.

Stern was a major supporter of reform candidates, including Mayor Chep Morrison in 1946 and Gov. Sam Jones in 1940, who appointed Stern chairman of the Board of Commerce and Industry.

But his influence over state government was even greater decades earlier. During the great flood of 1927, Stern, then chairman of the New Orleans Cotton Exchange, was one of the powerful business leaders who met in a bank boardroom and prevailed upon Governor Simpson to dynamite the levee in St. Bernard Parish.

Stern had seen power in Louisiana pass from the grip of the Bourbon elite to one-man populist rule—and he realized that neither would advance the state in the second half of the Twentieth Century.

The reemergence of Earl Long in 1948 convinced Stern and his associates that something bigger than another reform candidate was needed to get Louisiana government on track with that of other southern states in the postwar boom. He began exchanging ideas with other civic leaders about an organization to promote reform. They included attorney Monte Lemann, broker Darwin Fenner (a co-founder of Merrill Lynch) and attorney Lester Kabacoff, then first lieutenant of Stern's business enterprises and later New Orleans' premier developer.

They enlisted the involvement of dry-goods dealer Eben Hardie, who had a singular perspective on the excesses of the Long era. Hardie had been foreman of the blue-ribbon federal grand jury that investigated the Louisiana Scandals of 1939–40, resulting in the indictments of 145 people and the imprisonment of the governor and the president of LSU.

The genesis for the new organization would come from New Orleans, but the group itself could not. Around the state, long-smoldering resentment and suspicion toward the city, fanned by the Longs and other politicians, guaranteed that any statewide organization born in New Orleans would go no further.

So Stern and Kabacoff first contacted businessmen outside New Orleans who understood how state politics worked.

Cecil Morgan was head of Louisiana operations for Standard Oil Company, a prime tax target of Huey Long. In his earlier life as a state legislator, he had voted to impeach the Kingfish. The future dean of Tulane Law School (he would die in 1999 at the age of 100), like Stern, would remain in the background of the organizational effort while the manager of the big Esso Refinery in Baton Rouge, Col. Dan Spurlock, assumed the public role.

Sawmill owner Parrish Fuller of Oakdale nearly ran for governor himself in 1944 and 1948 before his wife and business partner talked him out of it. Though viewed by business leaders as a formidable potential adversary to Earl Long in 1948, Fuller nonetheless maintained a relationship with the Longs.

Huey Long would call Fuller on his trips through Oakdale and ask to meet him at the town drugstore. "The druggist would close the doors, and we would sit there and debate ideas suggested by Long," said Fuller, who later realized Huey was sounding out how his ideas would go over in the business community. Huey appointed him to the state Board of Education, to which he was later elected and served as president.

Fuller was a consensus choice to lead the new organization, but he declined for fear he could not devote adequate time to it. Instead, the critical leadership role of forging the idea into an organization would go to a Wisconsin native known as much for his eccentricities as for his entrepreneurial drive and talent.

Hugh Coughlin only slowed down for one meal a day—"he worked while others ate," noted a contemporary. His beverage of choice was tomato juice. "Or a martini," recalls Joe Smith, who remembered the intense but engaging and generous Coughlin as "a strange man and one of my best friends for years."

In 1938, Coughlin and two financiers took over a bankrupt string of icehouses that generated electricity and built it into Central Louisiana Electric Company. CLECO was one of the first private utilities in the country to use Rural Electrification Administration funds to bring electricity to remote homes and farms in central Louisiana and in the Florida parishes.

The company helped to diversify the Depression-ravaged rural economy by supplying power for the reviving timber industry. Coughlin would later lead the fight that resulted in a state severance tax on timber being substituted for the ruinous ad valorem taxes that could be manipulated by local assessors.

As head of the smallest of the state's investor-owned utilities, Coughlin had the political perspective and vital economic contacts without the baggage that would be carried by a big power company executive.

From around the state, other business leaders signed on: Ed Taussig, a Lake Charles car dealer; Frank Godchaux of Abbeville, who ran one of the largest rice mills in the state; Charlton Lyons of Shreveport, the longtime leader of the state's small Republican Party; attorney LeDoux Provosty of Alexandria; and Charles Manship, publisher of the *Baton Rouge State-Times* and *Morning Advocate*.

They did not have to invent PAR from whole cloth. There was a good example in New Orleans of what a nonpartisan research group should be and could accomplish. The Bureau of Governmental Research, founded in 1933 and supported by dues-paying members, employed a professional, nonpartisan staff to study municipal problems and offer solutions. BGR had originated plans to reorganize the city police and recreations departments and blown the whistle on the quadrennial practice of padding the city payroll at election time. BGR's impact was felt statewide when it uncovered facts that the federal grand jury used in investigating the Louisiana Scandals.

The Bureau laid the groundwork for a reform movement in the city that swept deLesseps S. "Chep" Morrison into the mayor's office. Perhaps a similar state organization could bring comparable results.

The Bureau of Governmental Research served as more than a model. BGR executive director Val Mogensen worked with Monte Lemann to develop proposed bylaws for the statewide organization. BGR picked up some early expenses, for which it later would bill PAR $467.20.

While there was early enthusiasm for the project, even an early consensus on a name and the nonpartisan nature of the organization, there was disagreement over its goals. Colonel Spurlock of Esso wanted an organization to press for lower taxes. Monte Lemann delicately argued in a 1949 letter that recommendations made by a nonpartisan research council ultimately "might result in lessening our tax burden, but that would not be the keynote, and the organization should not be one merely of large taxpayers, even though funds for its support must come largely from them."

After several temporary steering committees were unsuccessful at getting something started in 1949, the nucleus of leadership began forming the next year.

The organizational meeting was called for the Bentley Hotel in Alexandria on March 28, 1950. Sensitive to the notion that PAR had to be more than a business or taxpayers' group, Coughlin insisted that the invitational letters be signed by the presidents of the state's four independent colleges and universities: Centenary, Louisiana College, Loyola and Tulane.

Twenty-eight-year-old Joe Smith was among the 114 people, mostly businessmen and professionals, who gathered from around the state. "All present understood the gravity of the situation," recalled Smith. He said they also shared a common, and humbling, understanding: "Everybody realized how little we knew about state government. Unless we knew more, unless we had more facts, we were impotent."

Coughlin opened the meeting by comparing PAR to the Hoover Commission, which was formulating ideas for reorganizing the federal government. Charlton Lyons gave the keynote address. Former BGR director Lennox Moak, who would have been PAR's first director had he not taken a similar position in Philadelphia, gave background on how research organizations in large cities worked.

The group did not need much convincing. Monroe businessman Richard Kellogg made the motion to organize: "I do not see why we should not proceed right away." It carried unanimously. In short order, the bylaws Lester Kabacoff had drawn up for the nonprofit corporation were adopted. The nominating committee's slate of officers was elected, including Coughlin as president and Parrish Fuller as executive vice-president.

The resolve and spirit of the organizers impressed *Times-Picayune* reporter Ken Gormin, who described them as "men of good purpose" in the next day's lead story: "It was no longer New Orleans versus country, or country versus city, it was all for Louisiana, and the unanimity of opinion for the need was clear-cut."

PAR was born, though the executive committee decided two weeks later that operations should not begin until $50,000 to $80,000 was raised in dues. Coughlin and his colleagues were optimistic about finances. "We all felt that it would be a matter of only two or three weeks until the necessary funds were raised," he would later recall.

Not exactly. "This organization is rapidly going nowhere," Coughlin wrote to LeDoux Provosty two months later. Subscriptions totaled $21,925, less than half of what the executive committee agreed would be needed to begin operations. Coughlin still waited to be reimbursed for the $473 check he wrote to cover the luncheon at the Bentley.

PAR would need a jump start. Coughlin did not want to hire someone to lead a membership drive, reasoning that the organization would grow up around its professional staff instead of the broad base of interested citizens. Better to build around a core group of major givers in order to quickly discern if there was enough real interest to justify the research council. "It is one thing to give lip service to an organization to which you are subscribing $100 or $200," wrote Coughlin, "but it is a dead certainty that no firm is going to subscribe as much as $1,000 without then and there committing itself and its entire organization to give *active* support."

He pressed the officers to work harder to bring in major members. It did not happen in a hurry, but in October 1950, with 65 members and $43,425 in the treasury, Coughlin concluded it was time to begin looking for a staff and officers.

Most of the early members were drawn from Shreveport, Alexandria and New Orleans. Joe Smith described the charter members as "people who had independent means, to where they could not be gotten to. It was a tough thing when it started. Everything was so frontier."

That could have accounted for the disproportionately low participation from Baton Rouge, with its economy so tied to oil companies and state government.

The dues would come from business, but PAR's talent was fielded from the state's universities. One of its organizers, Dr. Robert French, took a leave of absence from the Tulane school of business administration to become PAR's first executive director. Other than a bank account, he started with only some furniture from a defunct foundation. He rented office space in the Triad Building on Third Street in downtown Baton Rouge.

Then French went to the government department at LSU to hire Dr. J. Kimbrough Owen, who would establish PAR's reputation for scholarly and unbiased study as its first director of research.

Next he hired 23-year-old Emogene Pliner, who had just received her master's degree in government from LSU. She would later become PAR's director of research and its senior staff member in years of service until her retirement in 1991.

More than anything, the new organization needed members. Finding them was the primary job description of the new director of public information, the 29-year-old assistant director of the Baton Rouge Chamber of Commerce, Ed Steimel. Within two years, the Arkansas native would be PAR's director and the public face of the organization for 22 years thereafter.

On the eve of publication of its first report in 1951, French described PAR to the *State-Times* as a "nonprofit, nonpartisan, nonpolitical organization" that would study "the finances and administration of state and local government."

French and Steimel crisscrossed the state speaking to any club and association that would schedule them. One issue of the *PAR Report* noted talks given to the Bunkie Rotary, the Alexandria Lions, the Monroe Traffic and Transportation Club and various citizens' groups from Ville Platte to Bee Bayou. Often Dr. French would speak in a city and Steimel would make a follow-up visit to recruit members. In its typical quantifying fashion, a *PAR Report* stated that in an 11-month period in 1951–52, staff members spoke to 108 groups totaling 8,932 audience members.

"I don't think there is a town in this state I didn't make a speech in," said Steimel, recalling his early experiences with the highway system. "You really have to work at it to get to Cameron. And Shreveport was a pretty tough ride then."

Some members went the extra mile to make French's and Steimel's count for more. After Steimel spoke to a group in Mansfield, state Rep. Johnny Rogers accompanied him down the main street. "We got nine new members in two hours and fifteen minutes," said Steimel, remembering Rogers fondly. "He leaned on them."

"How much does the state of Louisiana spend?" asked the Public Affairs Research Council in the first sentence of its first report, issued in May 1951. It was a good question, and no one in Louisiana had answered it until then. Using a federal census study on state finances, PAR concluded that Louisiana's $370 million in annual expenditures ranked tenth in the country and third per capita, while the state ranked 39th in per capita income.

Though the report was mailed out to only 300 members, PAR found a ready vehicle for expanding its audience in the state's newspapers, which gave the report coverage from the front page to the editorial columns. It was the start of a beautiful symbiotic relationship.

"It became a favorite of newspapers right away," said Joe Smith, who saw that firsthand at the *Alexandria Daily Town Talk*. "There was a dearth of any kind of factual information. No one had the resources to dig out data and pursue it and develop stories."

The young organization still trying to justify its existence finally had something to write home about. The next *PAR Report* to members noted, in typical detail, that stories and editorials on the first study were carried in newspapers with a combined circulation of 1,262,508.

Late in 1951, PAR shifted its focus from policy to politics with publication of its first best-seller, *The Voter's Guide to the 1952 Elections*. The volume hardly reflected the color and spice of a Louisiana election, but there was nothing else like it. It provided a calendar of election events, information on registering and voting, the functions of state and parish elective offices and brief biographies of state candidates.

As hard as the staff worked on researching, writing, fact-checking and preparing the publication for print, their real challenge would be to distribute the guides in time for them to do any good. In those days before permanent registration, voters had to register for every election a month in advance of balloting. Many citizens lost the opportunity to vote in the December rush. With the election guides rolling off the press less than two weeks before the December 15 deadline, PAR had little more than a press release to inform the public that copies were available for 10 cents apiece.

But once that notice ran in newspapers, the distribution problem turned into a frantic fulfillment challenge, as a torrent of orders poured in. All other business at the new offices on North Fifth Street was suspended as the research organization turned into a mail-order house to meet the crush of orders that climbed to 45,000.

In October 1952, PAR again broke new ground when it took on the most complex and forbidding feature of Louisiana government, the state constitution. The first *Voter's Guide to the Amendments* summarized and explained the 50,000 words constituting 34 proposed changes to the much-amended 1921 state charter.

"The amending process in Louisiana has heretofore represented an extreme form of minority control," stated a *PAR Analysis*. It noted that in past elections, "Amendments adding as much as $25 million debt to the state have been adopted with the approval of as few as 9 percent of the registered vote."

"We were dealing with so damn many amendments that no one could do any analysis," recalled Smith. He said the only information came from special-interest groups that would make the rounds in the state to sell their amendments to political bosses and newspaper editors. The best strategy for passage, said Smith, was "to try to get your amendment to the top of the list."

Easing PAR's distribution bottleneck this time were several of the state's major newspapers, which serialized the guide's analysis verbatim.

Though PAR took no stand on the amendments, the state's newspapers used the group's research to form their own editorial opinions. "Editors and publishers would call me and want to know if their positions were in line," recalled Steimel. Ultimately, the PAR analyses and newspaper editorials led to a new political phenomenon, a marked increase in the failure of amendments.

PAR seized that initiative to begin beating the drum for a new constitution. It would take twenty years, four governors and, finally, a wholesale voter revolt in 1970 that killed 53 proposed amendments before this recommendation was finally followed.

In a busy year for publishing, PAR inaugurated another popular mainstay, *The Citizen's Guide to the Legislature*.

Simply by profiling lawmakers, listing their occupations and religion and, very importantly, printing their photographs, the legislative guide put a face on the Louisiana Legislature. It stressed the point that citizens could contact their senators and representatives on specific bills. It used graphics very effectively with the introduction of its famous cartoon that still tells the story today: "How a Bill Becomes Law."

PAR members could track those bills through the *Legislative Bulletin*, published weekly during sessions. In eight editions covering the 1952 session, the *Bulletin* analyzed 803 bills, major and minor, dealing with issues ranging from Right-to-Work to a proposed stock law banning cattle, goats and swine from public highways.

With its three 1952 guides—to the elections, the Legislature and the constitutional amendments—PAR had made an impact on public awareness. Yet Hugh Coughlin and PAR's other directors were concerned that the research group was not getting to the core of the real issues of government. According to Joe Smith, the directors agreed that the organization was not consistently analyzing what the state was doing right, and doing wrong, and where it was spending too many resources, and too few.

Dr. French had assembled a top-flight research staff and set an example for accuracy, integrity and independence. Yet he had difficulty leading PAR to deliver timely, relevant research that confronted the pressing issues of the day. Nor could he balance a budget.

"Within eight months it was immediately apparent to the president and board. He couldn't cut it," remembered Joe Smith, who worked closely with Hugh Coughlin in PAR's early days. "Financially, it was a disaster, losing money hand over fist."

When French returned to Tulane in November 1953 to become vice-president of the university, there was no question who would be his successor.

Ed Steimel was summoned to Alexandria to meet Coughlin at his office along with Joe Smith and businessman Joe Pitts. Smith remembered, "He [Coughlin] became convinced that Steimel deserved a chance to see if he could do the job. He was young and untested and practically unknown, but a very persuasive salesman with a little fire in his belly. Eddie got the idea of what we were trying to do."

The first reality for Steimel to face was that he was the head of a nonprofit organization that was sinking in red ink. Though membership had grown to more than 1,500 and annual receipts topped $100,000, spending had swelled to over $120,000. Coughlin gave Steimel the job and a stern directive to do what it took to balance the books.

"That was my first introduction," said Steimel, who saw past the challenge to the opportunity to run his own show. "I did some trimming and I went to work raising money."

Within a few months, PAR's budget was back in the black,

owing more to Steimel's aggressive fundraising than to his cost-cutting.

Its financial outlook improving, PAR found state government moving again toward reform. And once again, the change was only partially due to the best efforts of conservatives.

Regardless of the names on the ballot, all elections since 1924 had pitted Longs against anti-Longs. But in 1952 the Longs would go to fighting each other. Unable to succeed himself, Earl Long chose Judge Carlos Spaht of Baton Rouge to lead the Long ticket. But recently elected U.S. Sen. Russell Long turned his back on his uncle, and joined Chep Morrison and Sam Jones behind a New Orleans candidate, Congressman Hale Boggs.

Another defection from the Long organization was Lt. Gov. Dodd, who angrily broke with the governor in 1951 when Long refused to back him in the upcoming race.

Less noticed in the intra-Long rivalry was the emerging candidacy of Judge Robert Kennon of Minden, who had narrowly lost the 1948 U.S. Senate election to Russell Long. Though Kennon was not a dynamic campaigner, his stature and demeanor attracted conservative voters looking for an honest outsider.

State Sen. Dudley LeBlanc was also running, despite an IRS investigation and a Federal Trade Commission injunction against his marketing of the elixir Hadacol.

Kermit Parker of New Orleans became the first African American to enter a Democratic primary for governor.

Lucille May Grace, the first woman to run for governor, filed a lawsuit to disqualify Boggs as a candidate because he was a sitting congressman. Plaquemines Parish boss Leander Perez, who hated Boggs, backed Grace until he switched his support to Alexandria cattle baron James McLemore.

Though he was the former mayor of Baton Rouge, Spaht was not a strong candidate. Governor Long did much of the talking for him, even promising to call a postelection special session of the Legislature to raise the homestead exemption if Spaht won.

But Long biographers Kurtz and Peoples maintain that the governor was not looking for a strong successor. The Louisiana Scandals, Long said, came about because "the boys stayed in power too long and they got too greedy." Indeed, defeat could be just the tonic for a political organization, as Long noted: "You let 'em lose an election and next election comes around they will be lean and hungry."

Long ignored Dodd and concentrated his invective on Boggs. Stumping in rural, Protestant North Louisiana, Earl savaged his opponent under the guise of defending him, as when he dismissed red-scare rumors about Boggs: "Why, he can't be a communist, he's too good a Catholic."

Nor did Uncle Earl spare Kennon, whom he labeled "Jug Ears." Long claimed, "They tested his blood and found it was 65 percent champagne and 35 percent talcum powder."

But Kennon connected with voters seeking a change. He not only carried North Louisiana strongly, but he also led in Baton Rouge. He shot into the second primary ahead of Hale Boggs and only 10,000 votes behind Judge Spaht. The second primary was hardly a contest as Kennon rolled up a 61 percent majority.

During the election, Long said state employees were "asked, not forced" to give two dollars each to Spaht. After the election, nearly 50 highway workers and state troopers, no longer protected by civil service, claimed they were fired because they did not contribute to Spaht's campaign.

Though PAR took no side in the election, it was closely aligned with Kennon on an agenda for changing Louisiana. His campaign platform read like a PAR handbook. He pledged to appoint independent blue-ribbon boards to run the big state agencies free from "cheap political pressure." Calling "the unlimited power of the governor" the cause of "most of the ills plaguing the state," Kennon promised "to not make it necessary for a legislator to make a trained seal of himself."

Kennon prevailed upon the Legislature to reinstate the civil service system that had been scrapped by Long, and to replace the last of the old ballot boxes with voting machines. He brought the state penitentiary at Angola into the Twentieth Century by correcting inhumane conditions and corruption.

His superintendent of State Police, Col. Francis Grevemberg, made a national name for himself by destroying slot machines and shutting down illegal casinos, which had flourished from Huey Long's regime to Earl's.

Kennon also pushed through a landmark piece of business legislation. The Right-to-Work law passed in 1954 ended the practice of forcing employees of a business with a labor contract to join the union as a condition of employment.

Though hailed by business, Right-to-Work had the unintended effect of rallying and unifying labor unions in the state. In 1956, the newly merged AFL-CIO elected its first state president, a Shreveport firefighters' representative named Victor Bussie, who would become the most prominent unelected official in Louisiana for decades to come. Bussie linked forces with PAR on early ethical reforms and the peaceful integration of public schools, but in time the labor leader would become PAR's, and Steimel's, most formidable rival.

With Kennon's support, the Legislature enacted one of PAR's earliest recommendations by establishing the Legislative Council to provide lawmakers with the most basic information on budgets, taxes and programs. Such information previously came only from the governor and his appointees, when they chose to give it.

The Legislative Council recognized PAR's pioneering efforts in research when it hired away three PAR employees, including Dr. Emmett Asseff, who became the Legislature's first research director.

The hottest political issue of the early 1950s was the state's burgeoning welfare system. To come to grips with it, Kennon and the Legislature requested that PAR undertake a comprehensive study of state welfare. The $80,000 project strained the young organization's resources. The final study revealed that 8 percent of Louisianians received public assistance, the highest rate in the country and double the national average, though Louisiana ranked 39th in personal income. Sixty percent of those over 65 received the old-age pension—three times the national average. PAR recommended lowering the limits on allowable assets for qualifiers and placing greater emphasis on rehabilitation for those with disabilities.

The study resulted in PAR's first national award by the Government Research Association. The Legislature, however, was less impressed, as it balked at the recommendations and shelved the report.

Through the 1950s, PAR pumped out studies on home rule, trade schools and charity hospitals, and complex analyses of financing highways and public schools. PAR studies of such controversial subjects were often attacked when not ignored by legislators and governors. But they were read about, both in PAR publications and in newspaper summaries, and would become part of the political and public discussion that necessarily preceded all reforms.

The Public Affairs Research Council was doing work that had not been done before. There was nothing else like it that used academic research to monitor the government's activities. That particular slant attracted scores of young people who were interested in making a difference in Louisiana government. In 1958, a graduate student's master's thesis led to a PAR study that blew the whistle on a massive land grab of oil-rich wetlands.

P. J. Mills was the first recipient of the PAR fellowship established in memory of Dr. Kimbrough Owen, PAR's first research director, who had died in a plane crash with the mayor of Baton Rouge in 1953. Having written his master's thesis on the state's levee boards, Mills expanded on his work in a PAR study of the seventeen flood protection districts.

Mills's research led him to examine the Wisner-Dresner contract of 1904, in which two New Orleans lawyers for the Atchafalaya Levee District devised a plan to pay 13 cents an acre for 900,000 acres of submerged land that the levee board had received from the federal government. The PAR study revealed that under the terms of the contract more tracts of levee board land were scheduled to be transferred to private hands that year. When the facts came to light, Governor Long issued an executive order to stop the transfer, and a special session of the Legislature rescinded the contract.

Few master's theses, or even PAR studies, have had such a tangible and immediate effect. Yet, as for PAR's policy recommendation that the seventeen levee boards be consolidated under a single state agency, said Mills, "It didn't have a damn bit of effect." The consolidation issue has been raised several times since in the Legislature, but all the levee districts remain in operation today.

"We had unbelievable freedom to research and publish without interference," says Steimel. That point was settled early on by PAR's first executive board, which overruled members wanting to reserve the final decisions on publishing conclusions and recommendations.

Such independence rested on the accuracy and fairness of the research. PAR developed a system of exhaustive checking and review, both inside and outside the organization.

Deciding what would be studied was the province of the research committee, the real center of activity for members who wanted to be involved in the group's work. Joe Smith remembers intense debates and interesting perspectives on what issues should be viewed as problems and which of those should be addressed. Attorney Ed Stauss of New Orleans chaired the research committee for years before becoming PAR president in 1971.

Once the executive committee scheduled and funded a study, the staff undertook the research and wrote a draft report. Copies went to the research committee and to any government body or industry affected by the study. "If they could show anything wrong, we changed it," said Steimel, who, as executive director, had the final say on the finished report.

That independence would face its sternest test in 1956 when a PAR study recommended the investment of hundreds of millions of dollars in idle state funds on deposit in banks, interest free. It was an enormous patronage tool for the governor, who could dole out the money as he wished.

The study indicated that other states were earning millions of dollars in interest on such funds, a point that did not go over well with the bank directors on PAR's executive committee. One telephoned Steimel to complain: "What idle funds? State funds aren't idle in my bank," he complained. "I have them all loaned out."

With banks threatening to pull their memberships if the study was released, Steimel called on then-president Ed Taussig in Lake Charles. The conversation was brief, according to Steimel.

"Can you back up what you say?" asked Taussig.

"Yes," answered Steimel.

"Then go ahead and publish it."

Indeed, 30 banks pulled their memberships, though one by one they came back. "It took sixteen years to get the last bank back," said Steimel, "but we did."

Prompted by the widespread publicity the report was given, reinforced by newspaper editorials, the Legislature passed and Gov. Jimmie Davis reluctantly signed the first idle-funds investment law in 1961. The law was strengthened during the McKeithen administration, and by 1975, PAR would report that once-idle funds accounts were earning $45 million a year in interest.

Heartened by Bob Kennon's reforms, many business and civic leaders, especially in New Orleans, were eager to see dynamic reform Mayor Chep Morrison run for governor in 1956. So was Earl Long.

"I'd rather beat Morrison than eat any blackberry or huckleberry pie my mama ever made. Oh, how I'm praying for the stump wormer to get in the race. I want him to roll up the cuffs, get out that little ol' tuppy and pull down the shades and make himself up."

As he did to "Sweet Smellin'" Sam Jones before him, Long attached a label to Morrison, "ol' Dellasoups," and noted that if he were to don the mayor's $400 silk suits, they would look like "socks on a rooster." That would become the title of an anecdote-rich biography of Long by Robert McCaughan.

Long's political organization, lean and hungry as predicted after four years out of power, mobilized for an all-out campaign. Money was no problem. FBI reports state that the Marcello organization gave Long $250,000 in 1956, and that Long returned the favor by pardoning several convicted narcotics peddlers. Long's self-professed bagman, David Bell, later told an interviewer that he collected hundreds of thousands more from sheriffs, legislators and other local candidates for the right to appear on sample ballots of the Long ticket.

Back in power, Long made short work of reversing signal achievements of the Kennon administration. The 1956 Legislature repealed the Right-to-Work law and dismissed the Kennon appointees to state commissions that were designed to dilute the governor's power. Yet recognizing that some fights would be too costly to win, Long made no move against constitutionally protected civil service.

Business leaders braced for another tax grab, which the new governor signaled in his address to the Legislature: "You read in the newspapers that Earl Long is pledged not to increase taxes, and I am, to a reasonable extent." He added that "sulphur, timber and the racetracks are not paying their fair share," and there would be more targets to come.

Long faced two new obstacles in his plan to raise more business and consumer taxes in order to expand his social programs. One was a new constitutional amendment requiring a two-thirds vote of the Legislature to increase taxes. The amendment passed by 50.2 percent in 1956, despite Long's vigorous campaign against it. Long calculated he could still meet the higher threshold in the Legislature, but he did not realize how hard a research organization would make it for him—his other new challenge.

Fortunately for Long, one area that Kennon had done little to change was the governor's control of the budget process, which still depended on executive control of fiscal information. The budget at the time was a complex maze of numerous funds supported by varying fractions of different dedicated taxes. Even finding all the various pots of money was a challenge.

Long justified his tax increase proposals with the low-balled projections of J. Harvey Rester, the commissioner of administration. The governor expected businesses to howl over the new taxes, but he had every reason to believe that the Legislature, backed into a corner by a projected budget shortfall, would comply.

Who would argue with the administration's numbers? Just making sense of them was nearly impossible. Taking up that challenge, PAR researchers found it difficult to get any cooperation from the bureaucracy.

As the figures were extracted from the administration, researcher Emogene Pliner pieced together a revenue forecast far brighter than that of the governor's budget office. Some figures were glaringly low-balled. In twelve of the sixteen funds, the administration projected revenue decreases despite substantial growth over the last several years. The budget office projected no growth in sales tax, while PAR predicted an 11 percent rise. The budget office expected a drop in personal income, but PAR saw a continued upward trend. The budget office planned for a decline in oil and gas royalties and bonuses, while PAR pointed out that the mineral revenue was setting new records each year.

Pliner dug deeper to uncover another $38 million in surplus funds lying in various state accounts. Then there was the $5 million appropriation for a Southern University branch in Lafayette that would not be spent because the Legislature voted to establish a New Orleans campus instead.

When her budget review was done, Pliner estimated that the state would run a $30 million surplus without the $45 million in new taxes sought by Long.

Concluding the unprecedented independent budget analysis, PAR criticized the Long administration for "unreasonably low estimates of revenue" and "incomplete data on status of surpluses in special funds."

With the tax package in peril, Commissioner Rester labeled the revised projections "fantastic" and ordered that PAR be barred from getting further information from his office. But the damage was done. The "34 Club," the one-third plus one members of the House that could now block a tax, were siding with PAR's figures over the administration's. By the end of the session, the governor's plans to raise taxes on natural gas, sulphur, timber and liquor were all defeated. Of his initial targets, Long was able to hike the tariff only on his favorite pastime, horseracing.

Earl Long literally did not know what had hit him. Attempting to lash out at the upstart PAR, he confused it with the new Legislative Council and vetoed the agency's budget. Its staff had to shut down the office and go home until the administration corrected the error.

But PAR was not yet in the clear. If it had overestimated revenues, as Long's aides claimed, the state would face a budget shortfall and PAR's reputation would be irrevocably marred. Indeed, PAR did err, but on the side of caution. Less than a year later, the state collector of revenue told PAR members at their annual conference that the 1956–57 surplus would top $44 million, $14 million more than Pliner had predicted.

Not that it stopped Long from trying the same thing again the following year. In 1957, he raised the stakes by linking the continuation of a teacher pay increase to a trebling of the natural gas severance tax.

Not only did PAR show that the pay raise could be met without added revenue, but it compiled, for the first time, a table of teacher salaries by parish. It was not easy. When Superintendent of Education Shelby Jackson flatly refused to cooperate, Baton Rouge attorney Payne Breazeale, PAR's pro bono counsel, briefed Steimel on the public records law. "I went to him [Jackson] with a law book in hand and said this is the information I want and you have three days to produce it or we go to court," recalls Steimel. "He stormed and raised hell but in three days we got the info."

With the House set to vote on the natural gas tax on a Monday, PAR rushed its report to the printer over the weekend and had a copy on each legislator's desk. The findings were stunning even by today's standards. In 1957, Louisiana's average public schoolteacher salary of $4,349 was the 16th highest in the nation.

The point was made. For years to come, until it formed the Legislative Fiscal Office in 1974, the Legislature would rely on PAR's revenue projections instead of the executive branch's in formulating budgets.

The 1956 confrontation was a defining moment for the Public Affairs Research Council. "Fundraising was easy after that," said Steimel. Annual revenue surpassed $200,000 in 1960 from a membership of 2,900.

Yet Uncle Earl could not be denied one last bite at the tax apple. In 1958, he broke the "34 Club" to pass a one-cent hike in the gas severance tax.

It was his last bite. Beginning that year, the governor of Louisiana began to fall apart. His heavy use of alcohol and prescription drugs, often in combination, aggravated the intense political pressure on Long as he tried to find room to maneuver between the federal desegregation mandate—buttressed by his own belief in civil rights for blacks—and the overt defiance of racist firebrands like Rep. Willie Rainach Jr.

Then came the wild episodes of Long's commitment to a mental institution, his self-discharge from a Louisiana hospital, a colorful road trip out west, his public cavorting with stripper Blaze Starr and, finally, a bald, futile attempt to keep power by running for lieutenant governor on a ticket with Jimmie Noe. Long gave up his harried bid in mid-campaign and retired to his pea patch farm in Winnfield. And once again, his enemies and many friends counted Earl Long out, again prematurely.

Six months after leaving office, a refreshed, reinvigorated Long roared back from political exile and hit the campaign trail against Congressman Harold McSween of Alexandria.

Late in the afternoon of the election day for the 1960 primary, Long's heart gave out. But he refused to be taken to the hospital until the polls closed, lest word get out. "I'd rather die in this hotel room than let that little c—— s—— beat me." He didn't. Long won his last election and died nine days later.

A great personal saga had ended, but an era had not yet passed. The enduring legacy of the Longs—a populist government controlled by a powerful governor—would hold sway in Louisiana for decades to come.

The governor's office would have been stronger still but for the growing flow of information that PAR was providing to the Legislature and the voters. For its part, the Public Affairs Research Council could claim in its first decade a few hard-fought reforms that were just beginning to introduce some balance to state politics.

In the decade ahead, PAR would be challenged to provide more than information. It would offer leadership also, as it found itself thrust into the center of a struggle that would change not just politics, but life in Louisiana and the South forever.

2

AGAINST THE TIDE

Like a weather report of a tropical depression in the Gulf, PAR's *Legislative Bulletin* of May 22, 1954, began with the brief note that the U.S. Supreme Court had just ruled in a Kansas case that segregation in public schools was illegal.

The full fury of the storm that would sweep the South, before heading north, was still several years in the offing, but PAR began right away analyzing the dubious stratagems and dangerous futility of elected officials sworn to defy the federal edict.

Ultimately, the question would not be whether public schools in Louisiana would be desegregated, but rather whether they would survive the political undermining of their public support.

Planted in the center of the action, PAR would advocate a consistent, if dispassionate, position of respecting the rule of law and supporting public education as a vital institution. Leaders of both sides in the emotional, wrenching debate would come to respect PAR's balance and objectivity, as evidenced by membership that included both Leander Perez and Archbishop Joseph Rummel, even after the latter excommunicated the former for preaching defiance of integration.

As in many other controversies, PAR came to recognize how the political structure, particularly the inordinate power of the governor, could hinder rather than facilitate resolution.

PAR had set its own house in order in 1952 with a unanimous vote of the executive committee confirming that membership in the organization was open to all races.

Starting in 1954, segregationist legislators introduced a series of bills aimed at circumventing federal desegregation mandates. Embattled proponents of public schools looked to PAR to objectively expose the measures' practical and legal shortcomings. When a legislator proposed a crash building program of schools for blacks, an attempt to mask a century of inequity, PAR noted that school construction was a local, not a state, responsibility. When a bill was introduced to provide state grants for children to attend private schools, PAR asked if the state intended to cover the tuitions of the 17 percent of schoolchildren already in private or parochial schools. It viewed skeptically another legislative attempt to invoke the principle of the "police power" of the state to enforce segregation in public schools as a matter of public order.

Its cold-eyed appraisal of the many emotional reactions to the new federal law aroused the enmity of some PAR members. Throughout the 1960s, Claiborne Parish remained a blank spot on PAR's membership map.

Black schoolchildren first walked into New Orleans public schools in 1959, but on the state level, the real battle was joined in 1960 when a federal court ordered the desegregation of schools in East Baton Rouge and St. Helena parishes.

Between those two events, segregation emerged as the dominant issue in the 1959–60 governor's race.

After Earl Long's internationally reported bizarre behavior of early 1959, the governor settled down to devise a scheme to hang on to power in the fall elections. His first trial balloon, to resign from office before qualifying to run again, so as technically not to succeed himself, was shot down. Then he announced he would run for lieutenant governor on a ticket with his friend, Monroe oilman Jimmie Noe. Suspicion was so strong that Noe, if he won, would immediately resign and turn back power to Long that the candidate publicly offered to post a performance bond with the state treasurer to ensure he completed his term.

It did not matter. Like Carlos Spaht before him, Noe was completely overshadowed by Long. And both were overshadowed by two other strong political personalities from opposite ends of the state: New Orleans Mayor Chep Morrison and former governor and singing star Jimmie Davis.

Further spicing up the race were former lieutenant governor Bill Dodd and state Rep. Willie Rainach. While Jimmie Davis would profess to be "1,000 percent for segregation," he came off as a racial moderate compared with the outspoken Rainach.

After the last tumultuous Long administration, the genial Davis offered the electorate "peace and harmony" but little else in his platform besides support for industry and opposition to integration.

With his huge name recognition, Davis became the target of other candidates scrambling for a spot in the second primary. Morrison called him "one of the laziest governors in state history." Bill Dodd said the previous Davis administration was "marked by do-nothingism and the peace and harmony of a well-kept cemetery." When Davis boasted of leaving office in 1948 with a $30 million surplus, Dodd shot back, "Anyone could have left as much if he did as little as Davis." And Earl Long claimed Davis' support for segregation was insincere because "he operated an integrated honky-tonk in California."

But Davis knew how to use his celebrity, his and others. His campaign placed an ad in the *Alexandria Daily Town Talk* in which LSU football star Billy Cannon posed with the candidate, prompting a claim by a minor candidate that Cannon had been paid $1,000 for the appearance. LSU and Davis denied it.

The first primary, held on December 5, 1959, marked the first time Louisianians voted on a Saturday instead of a Tuesday. The change at Long's behest, to "allow working people to vote," was unpopular among state employees, who were accustomed to having Mondays off before elections.

It would also mark the first time in seven elections that a Long or Long-backed candidate did not make the runoff, as Morrison led with 33 percent, followed by Davis at 25 percent and Noe running a poor fourth behind Rainach.

Though the runoff was billed as a city versus country contest, a decisive underlying factor was the support of organized labor. Whereas union power in the past had been concentrated in New Orleans, new AFL-CIO leader Victor Bussie, taking advantage of an industrial construction boom, had transformed his group into a statewide force.

He and Earl Long had prevailed upon the Legislature to repeal the Right-to-Work law four years earlier, but now it returned as a major campaign issue. The *State-Times* reported that a labor audience sat in "stony silence" as Morrison defended his stand not to veto a Right-to-Work bill if it passed the Legislature. Davis, he said, was promising both ways, telling the unions he would veto and then assuring the Farm Bureau and Associated General Contractors he would not.

When the union group endorsed Davis, Bussie told disappointed members backing Morrison that the mayor had refused to break his ties with the Teamsters Union, the aggressive rival of the AFL-CIO.

For the rest of the campaign, Davis would charge that his opponent was "the candidate of the NAACP and Jimmy Hoffa."

The newspapers predicted an exceedingly close finish, but Earl Long correctly surmised that the trend in the end was to Davis, who won with 54 percent of the votes in a record turnout of 79.9 percent.

Though he campaigned on peace and harmony, Governor Davis started his second term promoting political resistance to the federal desegregation mandate. At his back was fervent segregationist Judge Leander Perez of Plaquemines Parish, who arrived at the Capitol with placard-carrying demonstrators to keep up the pressure on the governor he had campaigned hard for.

The governor called five special sessions in the fall of 1960 to try to stop desegregation. In the first session, 29 bills to prop up separate-race schools were passed in record time. Following its policy, PAR did not advocate the defeat of any of the measures. It did not have to. In New Orleans, federal Judge J. Skelly Wright kept the court open late into the evening to strike down laws signed by the governor earlier in the day. The constantly shifting events were as confusing as they were extraordinary. Several times during the first session, the attorney general's office called PAR to verify what laws were still on the books.

But the governor of Louisiana could bring his own power to bear on the situation. In one special session, Davis pushed to increase the state sales tax by one-half cent to finance payments to parents who sent their children to segregated private schools. When legislators, armed with PAR research, questioned the soundness of the policy, Davis called their hometown bankers and threatened to yank deposits of idle state funds if the bankers did not pressure their legislators to drop their opposition.

Steimel said the president of the Louisiana Bank and Trust in Shreveport was "called upon to get legislators straight on the tax or lose $10 million."

The episode demonstrated how the deposit of state funds in non-interest-bearing accounts was more than bad fiscal policy. Besides losing money for the state, the practice gave the governor huge clout in other areas. PAR Associate Director Art Thiel explained, "The governor would call the bank and the banker would call the legislator and say, 'Hey, what are you doing?' It was a great deal to influence decisions on legislation."

With many business-oriented legislators sidelined, labor leader Victor Bussie took the lobbying lead and killed the tax.

Before Davis left office, the Legislature would follow PAR's recommmendation and enact the first law requiring the investment of state funds. PAR had not lost membership dues from banks in vain.

PAR was more direct in its opposition to the governor's unpledged-electors bill, which would have empowered Louisiana's electors in the next national election to shop for a deal with the Republican or States' Rights presidential candidate in return for a slowdown on desegregation. When no one else publicly objected, Steimel implored the president of the state bar association and the *Times-Picayune* to speak out against the move to disenfranchise state voters and to encourage legislators to kill the bill. When they did, some angry attorneys joined angry bankers in dropping their PAR membership.

As PAR's and Steimel's influence in shaping state policy grew, some inside and outside of the organization questioned whether Steimel was crossing the line and violating its prohibition on lobbying.

"That was the problem with a man like Steimel," remembered executive committee member Joe Smith. "Eddie could get so enthusiastic about what we discovered or uncovered that he couldn't help but stray from fact-finding and research to lobby for action. We always had to restrain him."

Some felt that PAR rather than Steimel should change. "There was a contingent that wanted to be more activist, even in the '50s," said P. J. Mills, an early staffer who would later serve on the executive committee. Though changing the group's role was debated at board meetings, members decided not to stray from the original mission of nonpartisan research. "We figured if we could do that job well, other things would naturally follow," said Smith. But would they?

The reluctance of politicians to realistically deal with desegregation demonstrated the need for an organization that could advance a public agenda. As with basic government reforms recommended by PAR, its leaders recognized that a wide gulf lay between nonpartisan research and political action. "There was so much [research] work out there, but no one was taking it and running with it," said Smith. "That was the genesis of CABL."

The stated purpose for the Council for a Better Louisiana was to advance the cause of business in government policy. But, according to Steimel, the underlying catalyst was the public school crisis and "Davis' attempt to wreck the state to overturn the federal courts."

As Edgar B. Stern had taken the lead in forming PAR, Edgar Stern Jr. laid the groundwork for CABL in a 1962 meeting with Lester Kabacoff, Steimel and PAR Associate Director Ed Stagg, who would be the first director of the new organization. Hugh Coughlin would be the first CABL chairman, as he was for PAR.

Though CABL was ostensibly a business group, its organizers recognized that a consensus for many broad reforms could not be achieved without the participation of organized labor. To secure the involvement of Victor Bussie, the founders tacitly agreed that CABL would steer clear of contentious labor issues, including Right-to-Work, workers' compensation and unemployment compensation.

With CABL providing a limited vehicle for lobbying broad policy issues, PAR would refocus on its original mission of nonpartisan, impartial research. There was so much still to be done.

PAR's challenge of the Long administration's revenue figures in the 1950s exposed the tangled web of budget funds and tax dedications that frustrated the Legislature's appropriation power. The budget morass was made worse by the growing labyrinth of state agencies, which swelled from 151 in 1951 to 217 in 1959.

PAR's repeated recommendations to undedicate revenues, reorganize government and write a new constitution all moved in the direction of giving more power to the Legislature. Legislators were starting to get the message.

On the last day of the first session of the new Legislature in 1960, the House of Representatives, over the votes of Jimmie Davis' floorleaders, passed a bill to strip the dedication of the major taxes, thus restoring some power of the purse to the Legislature.

State Rep. Eddie LeBreton of New Orleans argued that departments with dedicated funds could disregard the Legislature. "When you walk into the Welfare Department, they don't have to listen to you; they've got your money."

The *New Orleans States-Item* relished the landmark reform: "Some politicians expressed surprise when the Senate some days ago gave the measure a favorable vote; we assume they are now amazed."

The dedication bill would give new power to a new breed of lawmakers whom PAR would work with as well as contend with, such as the bill's lead author, state Sen. Michael O'Keefe of New Orleans. He would later become the Senate's first president elected by the body, and the most powerful legislator of his time, before the first of two federal fraud convictions drove him from politics.

Other key reforms that were early PAR recommendations found their way into law. In 1962, voters approved a constitutional amendment to establish the office of legislative auditor as a check on the executive branch. Since the 1950s, PAR had argued it was a fundamental flaw in the system for the executive branch to audit itself.

In 1963, the Legislature funded the first student loan program as a substitute for the legislative scholarships, doled out as political perks, that PAR had criticized.

Yet there was hardly a working relationship between PAR and Governor Davis, an old-style pol who did not understand why a group of citizens would get involved in government without expecting something in return. He particularly resented PAR's opposition to his efforts to avoid integration of public schools.

After eight years of Long and Davis, there was little interaction, even communication, between PAR and the governor's office. That was about to change in a way that no one at PAR envisioned.

In the fall of 1963, two candidates for governor held the promise of expanding reform initiatives that had barely edged forward under Jimmie Davis. Former governor Bob Kennon of Minden maintained a strong popularity among conservatives, especially in North Louisiana. Yet his avowed opposition to integration, highlighted by his personal animus toward President John Kennedy, worried PAR members concerned about the future of public education. So many of them rallied around the third straight gubernatorial campaign of former New Orleans mayor Chep Morrison, whom the president had appointed ambassador to the Organization of American States.

Kennon and Morrison and their supporters figured that Congressman Gillis Long, with his name and liberal Washington voting record, was the populist to beat.

Less regarded but not unnoticed was Public Service Commissioner John McKeithen of Columbia. PAR members well remembered the freshman state representative from 1948, immediately tapped as floorleader by Gov. Earl Long, helping to push through a raft of tax increases and the abolishment of civil service. Making him even less attractive, McKeithen the candidate seemed to have rejected his late mentor's racial moderation by pledging to fight to maintain segregated schools.

Given the ten-candidate field, a second Democratic primary between Morrison and Kennon would be the best of outcomes for those supporting the good-government measures recommended by PAR.

Morrison ran a modern, well-financed campaign that made strong use of the new vehicle of television advertising, so well suited to the polished New Orleans mayor. Yet the 1963 Democratic first primary would introduce Louisiana's first great television talent—just as Huey Long pioneered the radio—when John McKeithen rocked on a porch swing and delivered his homespun appeal: "Won't you please he'p me?"

His immediate challenge was to separate Congressman Long, a seventh cousin of Huey and Earl, from the Long vote, which McKeithen felt he was rightfully heir to. Dismissing "silly little Gillis," McKeithen ranted, "If Mr. Earl knew he using his name, he'd turn over in his grave."

The issue of segregation dominated the 1963–64 governor's race as it had four years earlier, but this time it was sharpened and personalized into intense opposition to the administration of President Kennedy and his upcoming bid for re-election.

When conservative candidates were not denouncing Kennedy, they were claiming other candidates were linked to him. McKeithen labeled Gillis Long "Kennedy's assistant whip," and Long shot back that McKeithen had campaigned for Kennedy in 1960. Kennon predicted he would be in a runoff with one of "the three Kennedy kids"—Morrison, Long or McKeithen.

An October poll showed Morrison and Long running comfortably ahead of McKeithen and Kennon. Kennon had entered the race late but was making up ground fast. A month later, McKeithen's and Kennon's anti-Kennedy rhetoric vaulted them into a tie for second ahead of Long. But McKeithen shrewdly focused on Long's ties to the administration and to passage of civil rights legislation while Kennon directed his attacks on Kennedy as though he were a candidate.

A newspaper column in mid-November credited Kennon with running a "smart campaign" on the day after he received the endorsement of arch-segregationist Leander Perez. In that same week, Gillis Long picked the wrong time to finally distance himself from the president. Claiming Kennedy forces had opposed his election to Congress, he said, "If I owe Kennedy anything, it's a good, swift kick in the pants." His statement appeared in the press on November 20, 1963.

Two days later, all candidates suspended their campaigns as the nation absorbed the shock of Kennedy's assassination. Overnight, candidates went from distancing themselves from Kennedy to distancing themselves from Kennon. The national tragedy "causes all of us to do a lot of soul searching," said a somber McKeithen, who nonetheless could not resist the jab: "One candidate has lost an issue."

Kennon, who fostered a Mr. Clean image, was also hurt by revelations he might have profited from a questionable state oil lease.

As his campaign collapsed and Long's stumbled, McKeithen moved into the breach as the reasonable, modern conservative alternative.

Chep Morrison led the first primary with 33 percent of the vote, just as in 1959. But his lead was wider, twice as many votes as McKeithen, who edged into the second primary fewer than 20,000 votes ahead of Long.

In the runoff with the more liberal New Orleans opponent, McKeithen could safely return to the racial theme that had helped beat Morrison the last time. With blacks casting 13 percent of first primary votes, most of them for Morrison, McKeithen warned reporters, "Louisiana faces a crisis because of the bloc vote." When he was surprised by reporters waiting for him to emerge from a secret meeting with Gov. Jimmie Davis, McKeithen recovered quickly and said he and the governor were discussing the disturbing concentration of black votes for Morrison.

The following week, the headline of a McKeithen ad in the *State-Times* announced: NEGRO BLOC VOTE FOR MORRISON. The copy detailed the lopsided votes for the mayor from selected black precincts.

Not that he was blaming black folks, McKeithen said: "I submit that the colored vote was delivered lock, stock and barrel by people outside Louisiana. They were not left alone."

Yet the younger McKeithen still had to demonstrate, especially to voters not preoccupied with the race issue, that he could match the stature of Morrison, a proven, capable leader with a national reputation. Few expected McKeithen to fare well in a debate with Morrison to be televised on WDSU. But the country candidate decided to combat style with substance. Shortly before the debate, someone handed McKeithen a PAR publication with a list of recommendations for changes in government, including the code of ethics the Legislature had rejected earlier that year. In a master stroke, he adopted the recommendations on the air as his reform platform, flummoxing Morrison, who had no prepared agenda to match them.

That episode may not have been the turning point in the campaign, but McKeithen's embrace of PAR's agenda secured his image as an agent for change rather than a throwback to Long populism.

Like Davis before him, McKeithen solidified his rural base and split off part of the New Orleans vote by appealing to the old political guard that Morrison had vanquished. He won votes on the West Bank by promising to take the tolls off the new Mississippi River bridge. Morrison supporters, many PAR members among them, felt a familiar sinking feeling early on election night when the New Orleans precincts did not come in strongly enough, followed by the wave of country votes that would sweep Earl Long's former floorleader into power.

Of all the governors before and since, John McKeithen had the most complex, stormy relationship with the Public Affairs Research Council. Unlike Earl Long, who wasn't always quite sure what PAR was, McKeithen took office fully understanding PAR's influence with the newspapers and opinion leaders crucial to his administration's success. Yet the dynamic, proud new governor did not take criticism lightly, especially when it complicated his plan to navigate a new middle ground in Louisiana politics.

Many in Louisiana, and in PAR, thought they had taken the measure of McKeithen. They were wrong.

Some expected the worst combination of the Long and Davis years, business tax increases and promises of segregation forever. But once in office, McKeithen became Louisiana's foremost economic developer and, with some political misgivings, defender of civil rights.

He developed the Right-to-Profit laws, a package of PAR-recommended measures that corrected longstanding tax inequities and put the state on a competitive footing with its southern neighbors. Then he embarked on a personal sales mission to recruit more large corporations, which led to an unprecedented industrial boom that transformed the economies of many poor parishes.

As a key part of opening Louisiana for business, McKeithen dropped the defiant racial rhetoric of the Davis years and committed his support for public schools.

He ordered or signed into law a number of basic reforms recommended by PAR but stalled in the Davis administration. The investment of idle funds was expanded, a master list of state employees was compiled and an inventory of public property was initiated.

McKeithen accelerated the pace of change that PAR had nudged along for years. As Art Thiel observed, "PAR would put out a report on some issue and there wasn't anything done. But by bringing it up periodically, the public began to think, 'This is a good idea.'" So too would candidates.

When PAR had recommended a code of ethics in 1963, many legislators had responded that rules for the conduct of public officials were not needed. But when a number of the same lawmakers were beaten by opponents using that issue, the Legislature reconsidered and passed the first ethics code in 1964.

As the first governor in many years to have served in the Legislature, McKeithen communicated well with lawmakers but was only willing to share so much power. Ultimately, the most effective check on a governor was that he could not succeed himself—a limitation that McKeithen was determined to remove.

Few legislators objected when McKeithen proposed a constitutional amendment to allow a governor to serve two consecutive terms. But PAR recommended that the change was premature, just as it raised doubts about the governor's plan to finance construction of a domed stadium in New Orleans.

Ed Steimel went beyond the printed word to criticize both ideas in a speech to the New Orleans Rotary, making inevitable the clash of two large egos.

When the phone rang at 6 A.M. at the Steimel household on January 20, 1966, it was not the governor calling to wish Ed happy birthday. It was the menacing voice of an enraged politician ready to rumble. "You've gone after my job. I'm going after yours,"

McKeithen said, according to Steimel. The two men argued for 30 minutes before both calmed down and hung up. But neither had the final word. Mary Steimel was so incensed that McKeithen had soured her husband's birthday that she called the governor back and gave him a very hot piece of her mind. A truce was not finally established until Marjorie McKeithen and Mary Steimel could have tea and straighten things out.

There would be more early-morning phone conversations between the governor and the PAR leader, but always in a more civil tone. As Ed Steimel recalls, "He never let a meeting pass without referring to what he was called by my wife."

McKeithen would continue to chafe at PAR's criticism of the administration's tax and spending policies and its aversion to reorganizing an unwieldy state government. He labeled a 1967 *PAR Bulletin* on the growth of the state payroll "mischief aforethought . . . [if not] . . . malice aforethought" as it was released a few months before the election. He complained that the report left the impression that "we have a bunch of deadheads on the payroll down here and that if it weren't for PAR on its white charger . . . a bunch of politicians in Baton Rouge would steal the state blind."

McKeithen took his next disagreement with PAR over Steimel's head and demanded of President Clifford Strauss that future publications be submitted to him before they were released. Strauss explained that only the executive committee could approve that action and that he would personally vote against it.

That PAR was an influence in state politics and yet not subject to the same political pressures as officeholders seemed to irritate the political class all the more. In dismissing a PAR recommendation to reduce the power of the governor by strengthening the Legislature, Lt. Gov. C. C. "Taddy" Aycock once told reporters, "If PAR's professional staff had to be elected instead of standing in the good graces of those who appointed them, perhaps their whole approach to Louisiana politics would be practical rather than professional and theoretical."

Differences with PAR did not deter McKeithen from successfully pushing passage of the two-term constitutional amendment, winning re-election with 80 percent of the vote and financing construction of the domed stadium with the proceeds of a new hotel-motel tax.

But the master of state politics was disillusioned when he tried to take his career to the national level. He went to the 1968 Democratic National Convention in Chicago as a self-proclaimed vice-presidential contender, but the view was not shared by nominee Hubert Humphrey and his national power brokers.

The disappointment would presage a rocky second term, but one that included McKeithen's finest moment when he activated the National Guard to protect civil rights marchers in Bogalusa. Not one to avoid the storm, McKeithen flew over the march in a state helicopter and watched angry whites in the crowd shake fists and shout curses up at him.

McKeithen started his second term at odds with PAR over a familiar topic, a proposed tax increase. PAR disputed McKeithen's cited needs for a $130 million tax package, which the Legislature eventually killed. In a special session, the governor dismissed PAR's suggested economies in state government, but legislators agreed with the group's numbers again and defeated all but a 1-cent gasoline tax hike.

A frustrated McKeithen fumed at Art Thiel, PAR's point man on the budget, when he encountered him in the Senate chamber. "You people let me down," said the governor according to Thiel. "I'm tired of good government."

Later McKeithen called Thiel with the challenge: "If you're so smart, why don't you come over here and do it yourself?" PAR took him up on the offer. The executive committee voted to allow its associate director to spend a year as a part-time, unpaid consultant to Commissioner of Administration W. W. McDougall.

From his first day on his new job, Thiel was "amazed" to find that "budget analysts were not used as analysts but as number counters. So I got them off that real quick." The executive budget would lump together what was needed to continue operations at the current level and what the department wanted for new programs. Thiel changed the process to separate "what we were doing and what we wanted to get done, so the governor and the Legislature could choose."

Following that endeavor, the governor, the Legislature and PAR would agree on a series of landmark reforms, including group health benefits for state employees, which was recommended by a 1964 PAR study and enacted in 1970.

PAR was well ahead of the curve in warning that the Legislature was going in the wrong direction on higher education, as it abandoned a network of two-year colleges in order to expand them to marginal four-year institutions with overlapping degree programs. A PAR study cited "poor planning and undue proliferation among the various public institutions." Its research revealed that one school offered 29 graduate degree programs, but only 151 students in all were enrolled. More than half of the junior-senior classes at one college and more than a third at another had five or fewer students.

Finally, in 1968, the Legislature created the Coordinating Council of Higher Education, but before the master plan could take effect, lawmakers also rushed through bills to redesignate six state colleges as "universities" and to authorize new degree-granting programs.

PAR's concern about state fiscal policy deepened as the growth of state spending outstripped even the booming economy. The McKeithen administration induced nostalgia for pay-as-you-go Earl Long. PAR revealed that in 1964–70, the state approved $1.247 billion in bonds, which was four times the $303 million authorized in 1950–63.

Responding to a *PAR Analysis* that exposed the problems of 25 state agencies issuing debt, not all backed by the state's full faith and credit, the Legislature followed PAR's recommendation to create a centralized debt-issuing body, the State Bond Commission, which led to a substantial improvement in the state bond rating.

Other reform issues proved too controversial for McKeithen to stay the course. He withdrew his support for equalizing property tax assessments after a committee he had appointed worked for 15 months without reaching a conclusion.

That encouraged some powerful tax assessors to resist PAR's requests for information on local assessment practices. Traveling around the state, Art Thiel time and again had to cite the public records law to make local officials cooperate. "A few wanted to run their own show," remembers Thiel. "Once they knew we had reference to the law, they were very cooperative."

Ordinary citizens seeking their own information from the tax rolls came to rely on PAR for its expertise on the public records law. Calls for help were so frequent that PAR published a wallet-sized "citizens' rights card" that spelled out the open meetings law and the public records law. Thiel still carries his.

Resistance to property tax equalization was finally broken by a federal court decision mandating uniform assessment practices. Yet the property tax issue as a whole and the efforts of powerful assessors in particular would continue to frustrate PAR staffs and fiscal reformers for decades to come.

PAR also differed with state and local officials on the appropriate level of support for public schools throughout the turmoil of desegregation. PAR took a broad view of race relations and economics with the 1967 annual conference entitled "The Impact of the Negro on Louisiana's Future." Though the tone of some of the speeches would now be considered patronizing, they made the point that the state could prosper only if all of its citizens could reach their full potential, which meant that barriers to equal opportunities had to be removed.

The meeting itself was something of a precedent; Steimel told the press that the conference luncheon marked the first time that many members had eaten a meal with blacks. And the last time, thought some. "We were told by our past presidents we were going to kill PAR with such a meeting," said Steimel.

But the conference was productive, as it led to a major PAR study on desegregation in 1969, a subject the state Board of Education had largely avoided even though fifteen school districts faced court-ordered mixing that fall.

The study began with the premise that local school boards had to proceed with orderly desegregation in accordance with the law. The findings dealt with how school boards could offset the gap in past educational opportunities between black and white students who would be attending the same schools.

The U.S. Department of Health, Education and Welfare responded to the report with a $62,000 grant to PAR to organize eight regional seminars to explain the recommendations to educators. Local school officials credited those meetings with diffusing many of the expected tensions of desegregation, which turned out to be less disruptive than originally feared.

For its efforts, PAR became a focal point of diehard but anonymous racist opposition. Some veiled threats were almost comic. A trio of professed Klansmen who came to the PAR office to protest its support of desegregation left sheepishly when Steimel informed them that Leander Perez was a card-carrying member. More ominous, and frequent, were threatening phone calls to Steimel's home at 2 A.M.

Nor was PAR's business side immune, beyond memberships dropped in protest. PAR field director Don Regan, whose organizing and sales talents boosted membership through the 1960s and '70s, experienced the hostility firsthand. He and Steimel once arrived at a membership drive meeting in Winnsboro in separate cars. When they left, they found identically worded messages attached to their windshield wipers: "The Ku Klux Klan has its eyes on you."

Yet the Klan's was not as piercing as the scrutiny of federal prosecutors and the national press on Louisiana politics. In 1968, the Louisiana Loan & Thrift scandal resulted in the conviction of Attorney General Jack Gremillion and six others. Two legislators were indicted and one was convicted. Dalton Smith was indicted for the attempted bribery of a governor's aide, but he was cleared. Then the state was rocked by a *Life* magazine story alleging organized crime influence in state government, even identifying a state official as the contact man for Mafia boss Carlos Marcello.

Ed Steimel fueled the fire in a 1970 speech to the Baton Rouge Rotary in which he condemned the Legislature for failing to outlaw pinball machines and offered his reason why: "The record makes clear that organized crime and organized gambling are well enough organized to exert unusual influence on the Legislature."

Called to explain his remarks to the Legislature's so-called Mafia Committee (formed after the *Life* exposé), Steimel came armed with research linking campaign contributions from gamblers to lawmakers' votes on pinball legislation. Committee members decided not to press the matter.

Steimel did not let it drop. He told the committee that a member of the Alcohol Beverage Control Board from Monroe was a partner in a company that placed pinball machines in bars under ABC jurisdiction. He backed his claim of illegal pinball payoffs by sending an LSU graduate student to several bars near campus to play the machines and collect winnings. He turned the evidence over to the Baton Rouge district attorney, but charges were never pursued.

If officials were turning a blind eye to Steimel's claims, others were not. In a wiretapped conversation played in a gambling and bribery trial in New Orleans, a pinball owner was heard to say, "I wish we could get the CIA to knock off two people, Kohn and Steimel." (Aaron Kohn was the head of the Metropolitan Crime Commission.)

Then Steimel shifted his focus to a scandal bigger than pinballs. The *Life* story alleged that organized crime's influence in the state

Department of Revenue enabled thousands of Louisianians, including public officials, to avoid paying state income taxes. The head of the income tax division had not paid taxes for years, and the attorney for the Revenue Department had not prosecuted anyone. Through his own sources, Steimel corroborated and expanded on the magazine exposé, feeding what he learned to local reporters. He estimated that $20 million a year was being lost in uncollected taxes. Years later, he would reveal that his primary source was a Revenue employee who attended the same church as his secretary.

The scandal led to the resignation of the top official in Revenue and, at PAR's recommendation, a law allowing the department to match state and federal tax returns.

Steimel turned over his gambling information to the U.S. Attorney's Office, which had been probing and later prosecuted several pinball machine company owners. Machines with "knockoff" devices that enabled illegal payoffs to be made were banned by the 1972 Legislature after they became a major issue in the 1971 governor's race.

PAR recognized that organized crime was not using muscle and bullets to get its way. The most powerful potential weapon to combat criminal influence in state politics had never been debated: public reporting of campaign contributions. PAR raised the issue and revisited it periodically, but two more governor's races would pass before even a weak disclosure law made it onto the books.

PAR's quadrennial *Citizen's Guide to the Legislature*, published after each election, had become the most useful reference for those who wanted to know who was making Louisiana's laws. In 1971, PAR served notice it would tell citizens even more about legislators with its upcoming pre-election guide to legislative voting records.

Art Thiel made casual reference to the planned guide in a speech near the end of the 1971 legislative session. On the next day, a resolution was entered in the House urging the Internal Revenue Service to investigate the tax-exempt status of contributions to the nonprofit organization. The resolution was beaten back, 25–60, and only served as advance publicity for what would become a PAR best-seller, with 35,000 copies of the voters' guide in circulation before the fall elections.

While some legislators fumed, most recognized that PAR was their strongest ally in the struggle to make the legislative branch more equal in power to the executive. A PAR recommendation had led to the formation of the Legislative Council in 1952, but its staff served only the key money committees. Analysts helped to draft the budget, but there was no analysis of the fiscal impact of regular bills, which could be substantial.

Individual legislators still had little more than their desktops to double as filing cabinets and offices. Former state representative P. J. Mills recalls, "We didn't even have phones at our desks. We had to go in the hall to use pay phones."

Nor did the House of Representatives in session resemble a body engaged in serious work. Decorum was wholly lacking as lawmakers ate at their desks, that is, when girlfriends weren't in their chairs with legislators sitting on overturned trash cans beside them.

But the comic scene ceased to be funny when a vote was called, as PAR reported in a wrap-up of the 1970 session: "Legislators' friends, relatives and even small children could be seen running from desk to desk voting legislators' machines in the House."

Even the great defender of due process, the American Civil Liberties Union, could not resist the temptation when a bill it supported came up. A *PAR Bulletin* quoted the state ACLU newsletter: "With our lobbyists on the floor pulling a number of voting keys for absent representatives, we got a majority."

But more than public confidence was damaged when the Legislature did not take itself seriously, as PAR had warned in 1965: "The Legislature in Louisiana has become far too weak a partner in the existing governmental structure of checks and balances." PAR suggested that legislators vote for improved decorum, adequate staff and facilities and the posting of notices of committee meetings, which not infrequently were conducted in hallways or bathrooms.

A group of first- and second-term legislators, the so-called Young Turks, banded together to have more input, especially on fiscal matters. They often turned to PAR for research and to Steimel for parliamentary and political strategy.

In 1972, under the leadership of newly elected Speaker of the House E. L. "Bubba" Henry, the Legislature would change its procedures for doing business. But first, Steimel and PAR would play a lead role in restructuring the Legislature itself.

For years the Legislature had turned a deaf ear to PAR recommendations that it reapportion itself to reflect population shifts away from the city of New Orleans and rural parishes toward growing urban and suburban areas. Finally, U.S. District Judge E. Gordon West ordered reapportionment in line with the Supreme Court's sweeping "one-man, one-vote" edict.

Yet it was more than even a federal judge could do to make legislators redraw their own districts. The Legislature tried once, but the U.S. Justice Department rejected the gerrymandered effort to protect incumbents. With the fall primaries approaching, the matter was left to Judge West, whose last option would be to order all state senators and representatives to run at-large statewide.

But a brief lunchtime encounter averted that and put the leader of PAR in charge in one of the most sensitive endeavors in the history of state politics. Judge West and his staff ate regularly at the old Piccadilly Cafeteria on Third Street. So did Steimel and PAR colleagues. Steimel stopped at the judge's table one day and casually remarked he would be happy to help in any way he could with the reapportionment problem.

A few days later, the judge called Steimel to ask if he would agree to become the special master to draw new district lines for the Legislature. Steimel tracked down PAR President Edward Stauss, vacationing in Florida, who gave the go-ahead, with the proviso that Steimel accept no pay from the government.

It was August 6. Judge West wanted a finished plan in 30 days. The first primary was set for November 6.

Though court rules required that an individual, not an organization, serve as special master, the landmark reapportionment plan of 1971 was a total PAR effort behind Steimel's leadership. Of all the studies, analyses, guides and recommendations issued by PAR in twenty years, none had ever been backed by the force of federal law. Even so, never had the staff worked on so important a project on such a tight deadline.

Steimel and Thiel set up four days of hearings, at which they conferred with 85 members of the Legislature and over 40 other individuals and groups, including the plaintiffs in the pending case.

But the real work came down to maps and numbers. To say the redistricters started from scratch was no exaggeration. Emogene Pliner began urgent calls to clerks of court for maps showing precinct lines. In more than one case, the only such record hung on the wall in the courthouse. Pliner had to persuade clerks to take down the maps and mail them special delivery.

The task would go beyond drawing new lines. Though it was not specifically mandated by the court, Steimel determined that single-member districts would replace a system that included some multi-member districts in large parishes. The old system gave a big political advantage to labor unions, which could concentrate their votes to elect slates of labor candidates in larger parishes. Business interests were not as organized to win elections . . . yet.

Multi-member districts also posed barriers for blacks and Republicans running for the Legislature. Vic Bussie of the AFL-CIO would argue that blacks might gain representation but would lose broader influence over white legislators who had to respond to minority constituents. The minorities did not buy it. The NAACP and the state Republican Party intervened in a federal lawsuit on the side of plaintiffs demanding single-member districts. The AFL-CIO would fight the suit on appeal.

PAR, meanwhile, had a deadline to meet. Working with census maps obtained from Louisiana Tech, cross-referenced by parish maps showing wards and precincts, 23-year-old researcher Reilly Stonecipher began putting together the pieces of the political jigsaw map. Besides heeding the court-ordered maximum deviation of 2 percent, Stonecipher took extra pains not to divide districts by large natural barriers, like rivers and swamps. He also tried to avoid putting a small section of one parish into a district dominated by voters in a larger neighboring parish.

Of less concern was placing two or more incumbents in the same district, which was all but unavoidable. "It wasn't part of my job to protect incumbents," said Steimel.

Unlike in future court-supervised reapportionments, the racial mix of districts was not taken into account. Yet simply drawing logical single-member districts offered the first opportunity for black voters in Baton Rouge, Shreveport and Monroe to send their own representatives to the State Capitol. In 1968, Ernest "Dutch" Morial of New Orleans had become the first African American elected to the Legislature since Reconstruction. After reapportionment, eight black representatives would enter the Legislature in 1972, joined by another emerging minority, four Republicans.

After fourteen days of intensive work, staffers piled bundles of maps and documents into the back seat of a car and delivered them to Judge West at the federal courthouse. Judge West signed off, and after adjustments to two New Orleans districts were made at the appellate court, the historic remap of the Legislature was complete.

Legislators, predictably, were outraged, though the ones who were the maddest, of course, were those least likely to return. "We were roundly condemned," recalls Steimel. "But I told our staff that as soon as the election was over we would have a lot of friends," namely, the legislators elected in PAR-drawn districts.

The move to single-member districts marked a fundamental change in Louisiana politics, one that brought the House of Representatives closer to the people, and made PAR's job easier.

As construction delays increased and costs on the Superdome soared, Gov. John McKeithen's popularity sagged in the last years of his second term. Sensational allegations of organized crime's influence tainted the good-government reputation of his administration. His relationships with the Legislature and the press soured, and he was barely on speaking terms with PAR, which he now labeled "a complete, negative organization." To a new generation of voters, McKeithen, elected eight years earlier as a reformer, now symbolized old-style politics far out of step with the changes sweeping both government and society.

Much of the public dissatisfaction could be expected for any political leader holding power so long during the tumultuous 1960s and early '70s. History would treat McKeithen better than would the critics in his own times. He would be seen as a responsible leader who confronted the strong segregationist sentiments that threatened public education, as a dynamic promoter whose aggressive salesmanship attracted billions of dollars of industrial development to the state, as the visionary builder whose Superdome would reinvigorate the New Orleans tourism industry.

John McKeithen: builder, promoter, leader, but not a reinventor of government, and surely no policy wonk.

McKeithen's focus on the big picture caused him to overlook a swelling bureaucracy in bad need of streamlining. It could be that the survival of his big projects, particularly the Superdome, required that he accommodate the political status quo rather than rock the boat. Whatever the reasons, though McKeithen started out by vastly improving on the record of the Davis administration, he was destined to leave office with an unfinished reform agenda of his own.

McKeithen pushed for a code of ethics in 1964 but did not press the Legislature for meaningful campaign finance disclosure laws. Nor did he forcefully support a bill to outlaw pinball machines in 1970. In his second term, he clashed with PAR on its opposition to his tax bills and on his refusal to cut the growing state payroll.

Though McKeithen followed a PAR recommendation to eliminate local agent commissions by coinsuring state buildings, a 1973 federal trial of a former McKeithen aide would reveal that select legislators continued to collect agent commissions of $10,000 or more.

The governor never heeded PAR's call to stop the appointment of attorneys to assist in the collection of inheritance taxes, a patronage plum that could enrich chosen lawyers by $10,000 a year in small parishes and up to $100,000 annually in New Orleans. The 64 patronage jobs would not be eliminated until 1974.

Through the 1960s, PAR urged the end of another blatant patronage practice: tax discounts to distributors of beer, whiskey and tobacco that were double and triple those paid by other states. The money from the excessive discounts formed a patronage pool that politicians, from governors to legislators, could expect to flow back to them in the form of contributions (unreported, of course) at election time. Bills to eliminate or reduce the discounts were filed annually but never made it out of committee in the McKeithen years.

PAR had identified the governor's selection of architects and engineers as another prime source of patronage, but the practice would continue until 1975.

Studying the imbalance of power in state politics, PAR had warned against the pervasive practice of the governor filling vacancies on local school boards, police juries, city councils and especially the judge's bench. Once appointed, those officials had a strong advantage when the next election occurred. In effect, governors were appointing judges for life, which made a mockery of the separation of powers. Gradually, the Legislature returned control of local offices to local voters through provisions for special elections. But the appointment of judges would remain the province of the governor until the new state constitution took effect in 1974.

And that was the little stuff. McKeithen never pressed for a new constitution, which swelled more in his two terms, nor for a consolidation of state agencies, at 264 and counting by 1971.

Eventually, the people took matters in hand. Assisted by PAR guides, which were well covered by the newspapers, voters were growing more selective in approving amendments. Before 1960, more than 80 percent of proposed amendments were approved, but only 60 percent afterwards. Finally, in 1970, the Legislature went too far when it sent a record of 53 proposed amendments to the voters, who defeated every one of them.

By the fall of 1971, with a revolution of lifestyles reshaping America, the state was ready for big changes of its own: a new Legislature, a new constitution and a new governor, one unlike any seen before.

3

MEET THE MASTER

The mandate for change was almost palpable in the governor's campaign of 1971. Yet, at its start, the better-known of the seventeen candidates were names from the past. Former governor Jimmie Davis and Congressman Gillis Long, both veterans of gubernatorial contests, were early favorites. Lt. Gov. C. C. "Taddy" Aycock and state Sen. John Schwegmann of Metairie, the discount grocery magnate, had built-in followings. And if one Long was not enough, Congressman Speedy Long, who had unseated Gillis in 1964, entered the race too.

Two other candidates seemed more attuned to the changing political times.

Congressman Edwin Edwards of Crowley, though little-known statewide, began with the most organized campaign and a solid geographic and cultural base among French and Catholic voters in the southwest. The charismatic candidate was also the subject of the most personal rumors. *State-Times* columnist Jack Lord noted that at one early appearance, "Edwards showed off his wife to dispel rumors that she is leaving him."

Late in the primary, a 39-year-old state senator from Shreveport, J. Bennett Johnston Jr., emerged to challenge Davis and Long as the leading North Louisiana candidate. Johnston connected with affluent and better-educated voters across the state, including many PAR members, who were looking for a true reform candidate in the absence of the late Chep Morrison. Johnston also had a following on college campuses in this first election in which 18-year-olds could vote.

In style and substance, Edwards and Johnston, both attorneys, represented a break with the candidates of the past. They both made corruption in government their centerpiece issues, while former governor Davis and Lt. Gov. Aycock emphasized the subject least. They both embraced a long list of recommended PAR reforms that had gone unaddressed, especially the need for a new constitution and the consolidation of state government.

Edwards estimated that the 267 state agencies employed about 225 purchasing agents, which "opens the door for illegitimate purchasing agreements and . . . kickbacks and fraudulent schemes." Johnston proposed a Louisiana Bureau of Investigation to root out corruption in government.

Of course, no Louisiana election can do without some pie in the sky. When Edwards said he would build a new bridge across the river in New Orleans, Speedy Long came behind him and promised three.

On election night, the changing dynamics of Louisiana politics were revealed, beginning with the collapse of Jimmie Davis, who finished a poor fourth despite his courthouse gang support. The other powerhouse to fall short was Gillis Long, who came in third after losing Long votes to cousin Speedy and many black votes to Sam Bell, an African American from New Orleans.

Edwards commanded the strongest base, carrying 22 parishes, all in the "Cajun triangle" of South Louisiana, to lead the Democratic primary with 23.5 percent of the vote.

The surprise of the night was "Bennett Who?"—as many voters asked—when Johnston's late surge pushed him ahead of Long and into second place, with 17.5 percent. As his young supporters chanted, "When you're hot, you're hot," the beaming Johnston took the stage as the candidate of momentum.

The second Democratic primary—at this time always the decisive contest—would become a Louisiana classic, the closest and perhaps most consequential governor's election of the century.

In those days before campaign finance laws, huge sums of money flowed into both campaigns, with no limits on individual contributions and no disclosure of sources. Johnston had introduced a campaign disclosure bill that year, but it did not get out of committee.

Edwards campaign aides remembered stacks of cash on a table in the Monteleone Hotel suite where brother Marion Edwards worked the phones for more. As the candidate would later recall, "We sat in that hotel room and raised thousands of dollars in the morning and gave it away in the afternoon and the next day I couldn't tell you where half of it came from or went."

Edwards did not let his promises of reform get in the way of traditional runoff deal-making. The congressman moved quickly to strike alliances with the sheriffs and courthouse gang that had been with Davis and Aycock. But the real prize was the endorsement of third-place finisher Gillis Long, who had won the black vote statewide and carried Orleans Parish with the help of an impressive get-out-the-vote effort by the new political organization SOUL.

"Gillis Long got us in a bidding war," Edwards would recall 29 years later during a break in his federal racketeering trial. "His endorsement was not as important to me as he would have been to Bennett Johnston," who needed help in attracting black votes.

Long was not greedy. He wanted help in retiring his campaign debt, the next governor's support in his planned race for Congress and, in the meantime, a job as director of the new Louisiana Offshore Oil Port.

Some of Johnston's younger aides wanted to jump at the offer, but senior advisers insisted he stick to his nickname of "No Deals Bennett." When Johnston passed, Edwards quickly made the deal that likely made the difference.

Late in the second primary, nonpartisan PAR found itself embroiled in the controversy over the sensitive issue of property tax assessments. A court had ruled that parish assessors must assess all property within a class at the same rate, but the Legislature had failed to enact an equalization law. Edwards ran an ad accusing Johnston of supporting the 100 percent assessment of property by his vote against a 1971 bill in the Legislature. When a reporter asked PAR Associate Director Art Thiel about the bill, he said that Edwards was mistaken about the effect of Johnston's vote. He said the bill Johnston opposed, to require 25 percent assessment, was badly flawed and would have legitimized existing tax inequities.

When Thiel's comments were widely reported, Edwards angrily accused PAR of taking sides and said it "should address the facts and let the candidates handle the campaign." Said Edwards of Thiel, "The gentleman is guilty of practicing law without a license and he is wrong in his interpretation."

On the third day of press coverage, Ed Steimel was forced to publicly restate PAR's neutrality as he tried to extricate the group from the roiling campaign controversy.

After 50 years of governor's races turning on the Long versus anti-Long axis, the 1971 campaign became a north versus south contest. While Johnston argued against sectionalism, Edwards, from the more populous south, exploited the geopolitical divide by pointing out that every governor since Sam Jones in 1940 had come from North Louisiana.

Leading in the polls and predicting a 55 percent victory, Johnston decided to go south to campaign in the bigger parishes in the final two weeks of the race. That may have cost him the election.

Had Johnston stayed at home in the final week, he may have boosted turnout in his base, where many of his likely voters, confident of their man's victory, disappeared into the woods for the opening of deer season on that first November weekend. That, or Gillis Long's endorsement, or any of a half dozen other factors, could have helped Johnston to hold off the resurgent Edwards' campaign.

Johnston carried 38 parishes, sweeping North Louisiana, Baton Rouge and the Florida parishes and splitting the New Orleans area. Though Edwards carried only 26 parishes, and none of the 4 largest, his huge vote in rural South Louisiana spelled the difference. In the closest governor's election in state history, Edwards won by 4,488 votes, 50.2 to 49.8 percent.

Turnout made the difference. In a postelection analysis, PAR calculated that of the 10 highest-turnout parishes, Edwards carried 8, all in Acadiana. Of the 24 parishes with the lowest turnout, Johnston led in 21, including his home parish of Caddo, which ranked 60th in voter participation. The broadly defined Acadiana region held 27 percent of the voting-age population but accounted for 33 percent of votes cast, of which 68 percent went to Edwards.

No wonder, as late returns poured in from the Cajun Prairie, that Edwards stood on a chair in the ballroom of the Monteleone Hotel and shouted, "Let's give three cheers for the coonasses."

But he also knew to credit another ethnic group. He next pulled up on the chair Nils Douglas, the president of SOUL, and announced, "Without this man we would not have won." In the first open governor's election since the passage of the 1965 Voting Rights Act, blacks cast 22 percent of the votes, up from 13 percent in 1963. By far, most African American voters went with Edwards, and would stay with him, more loyally than even the Cajuns, for the rest of his long career.

Though the second Democratic primary was the decisive election, it was not the final one. After two expensive, exhausting primaries, the Democratic nominee still had to face a fresh and well-financed Republican opponent, David Treen, in the general election. Only 5 percent of the state's voters were Republican, but Treen's support was swelled by Bennett Johnston backers who would rather cross party lines than vote for Edwards.

Edwards prevailed with a 57 percent majority but was nonetheless angry at having to win three elections. He vowed that no future governor, himself included, would have to go through that ordeal again. Two years later he kept his promise when he signed the open primary law, the unique nonpartisan election system that would serve Edwards well.

Edwards took office still blaming PAR for having sided with Johnston on the property assessment controversy. He began by ignoring the group, but he was too good a politician to let election grudges limit his effectiveness. He summoned PAR's top officers to the Governor's Mansion in 1972 and aired his grievances. But then he concluded that while his approach had to be more political than PAR's, he agreed with the research group on too many thorny issues not to keep open the lines of communication.

PAR leaders came away with a respect for and an assessment of the new governor that would be echoed by many, friend and foe, who would deal with him over the next three decades in which he dominated Louisiana politics. Art Thiel stated, "When we came out with something that was critical [of his administration], he would call up and we would sit down and talk about it. . . . You could talk to him and he would say yea or nay and you could count on it."

Results-driven businessmen had to admire Edwards' management style, which was long on delegation and short on details. He did not sit on decisions, once telling an aide, "Half of my decisions are right. A quarter could go either way, and a quarter are wrong. But you can adjust them later. The important thing is to keep things moving."

Before even taking office, Edwards started moving state government toward some of PAR's major reform recommendations. Addressing a PAR conference before his inauguration, he promised to tackle government reorganization and a constitutional convention: "Reform is around the corner. Either you lead or you follow, or you stand aside. Because it's not going to stay the same."

The Legislature already had changed. The combination of reapportionment and widespread voter dissatisfaction spelled bad news for incumbent legislators, only 40 percent of whom returned in 1972.

True to his campaign pledges, Edwards urged the new Legislature to adopt long-waiting reforms. Pinball machines with payout devices were outlawed (and the ban enforced by new State Police commander Don Thibodeaux). The appointment of attorneys to assist inheritance tax collections was stopped, as was the practice of assigning commissions for insuring state buildings. Tax discounts for liquor, beer and tobacco wholesalers were brought in line with those in other states. When the Legislature failed to set up architect and engineer selection boards, Edwards signed an executive order doing so.

Policy moves aside, what captured the public's attention was their new governor's style, every bit as flamboyant as that of Earl Long and, like Huey Long's, *sui generis*. Edwards was fast with repartee, and even faster to flirt with attractive women, whom he frequently propositioned. He once told this writer, "Two out of ten women are willing to go to bed with you but you have to ask the other eight."

The public soon learned that the governor was not only a gambler but a high roller, one whom Nevada casinos would send their planes to pick up. "None of your goddam business" is how he responded to one reporter's query about a gambling trip as he stepped off a casino's plane in Baton Rouge.

But the FBI considered it their business when questions about who settled Edwards' gambling debts led to their opening of the first of more than two dozen federal and local investigations, by Edwards' count.

Despite his fast lifestyle and constant controversy, Edwards delivered on his major reform promise when the Legislature, at his urging, called a convention to write a new constitution.

Louisiana's 1921 charter, originally less than 50,000 words long, had been amended 536 times in 51 years, ballooning to 255,000 words. It was not only the longest of any state but, according to PAR, the longest of any nation save India.

Recognizing the time was coming, PAR in 1970, the same year voters rejected all 53 amendments placed before them, published "A Procedure for Revising Louisiana's Constitution." It set up a speakers' bureau, with legislators among its 25 members, who urged the need before civic groups for a constitutional convention. When the convention was finally called, the governor appointed Steimel to serve on a five-member planning committee.

After the election of delegates by legislative district and the appointment of twenty more by the governor, Constitutional Convention 1973 got under way in the cavernous Independence Hall near the State Capitol.

The body of 132 delegates, who were paid $50 per diem, was as illustrious an assemblage of political personalities as the state had to offer. They included: 40 legislators, from civil rights leader Avery Alexander to idealistic conservative Woody Jenkins to Earl Long's old floorleader Sixty Rayburn; future Speaker of the House John Alario and future Senate President Sammy Nunez; counsel to three governors Camille Gravel; two future candidates for governor, Louis Lambert and Jim Brown; and one future governor, Buddy Roemer.

They also included: Supreme Court Justice Albert Tate and two future federal judges, Tom Stagg and Jim Dennis; business leader Donald "Boysie" Bollinger and leading trial lawyer Wendell Gauthier; six mayors; and one very powerful assessor, Lawrence Chehardy of Jefferson Parish.

Delegates Chalin Perez of Plaquemines Parish and Lynn Perkins of Catahoula Parish would later marry. So too would Buddy Roemer and Patti Crockett, then a 19-year-old convention page.

E. L. "Bubba" Henry, the former Young Turk who had become Speaker of the House, was elected chairman of the convention.

As might be expected, PAR upset the harmony. Eight months into the year-long convention, the research group took attendance with its booklet "Is Your Delegate Voting?" Fourteen delegates had failed to do so half of the time, while one, Dick Guidry of Lafourche Parish, amassed a perfect record, not one recorded vote. The usual denunciations of PAR ensued as delegates defended Guidry, who said "PAR can go to hell" before resigning from the convention.

PAR assigned eight staff members to follow the convention and spent $165,000 publishing sixteen analyses of its work. Though the analyses were often attacked, PAR research played a significant role in framing the final constitution.

By late 1973, Ed Steimel and the PAR staff became troubled at the direction the convention was taking on key issues, and Governor Edwards responded. The staff prepared a special critique of completed articles that focused on weaknesses and suggested corrections. Instead of going public, it gave copies only to the governor and Chairman Henry. Edwards selected half of the twenty recommendations and went before the convention to urge their acceptance. Most were adopted.

But on key points, especially civil service, education and property taxes, PAR recommendations were not supported by the governor or the convention.

PAR considered the civil service provision too detailed and inflexible for future legislatures to adjust. It deplored the compromise creating five boards of education as unwieldy and counterproductive. It was concerned that a specific prohibition of public aid to private schools was not included. It also warned that the loose language mandating the Legislature to "define and suppress gambling" was a loophole in waiting.

Yet Steimel, who attended all sessions of the convention, was most alarmed when the delegates left personal income tax rates in the constitution while taking corporate tax rates out. This would enable the Legislature to raise corporate taxes by statute, which it would later do, while raising individual tax rates would require a vote of the people. Also, the convention would shift a greater burden of local property taxes to businesses by allowing the Legislature to raise the homestead exemption from $35,000 to $50,000 (at the time, only military veterans qualified for the top exemption). Steimel said of the framers: "Just the middle class made up the convention and they wrote the article to suit themselves."

When the convention's work was done, PAR's staff and executive board concluded that the final document contained more bad than good. Though it showed many improvements over the 1921 charter, Steimel said, "The overwhelming thing was that it was detrimental to the creation of jobs and to the poor who carry the burden of taxes."

PAR was bound by its bylaws not to take a position, but few who heard any of Steimel's speeches on the document doubted where he stood. As part of the group's speakers' bureau, which discussed different sections of the proposed constitution, Steimel chose to focus on the finance section, on which he had little good to say. "The finance article is, by far, the worst article adopted by the convention," he told the Baton Rouge Chamber of Commerce. "This is one of the biggest things that is going to close the door on economic growth in this state."

Following similar remarks in Lafayette, the executive committee heard complaints that PAR was out to torpedo the whole constitution. Steimel defended his position but agreed to balance future remarks by noting positive features of the work.

Still, when the Shreveport Chamber of Commerce voted to oppose the constitution after Steimel addressed the group, Governor Edwards responded by attacking him in a speech to the AFL-CIO state convention in Baton Rouge.

"I don't think we need any carpetbaggers from Arkansas coming here to tell what the people of Louisiana stand for," said the governor of the PAR leader. "Obviously he is a white man because he speaks with forked tongue."

Warming to the labor crowd, the governor promised to organize volunteers to picket the businesses of PAR members so the public would know "they give money to people who say we are no good." And for good measure, he added, "You know how to get the *Shreveport Times* and the *Times-Picayune* and PAR to endorse the constitution in a New York second? All we have to do is add a paragraph that says labor unions are outlawed."

Though a majority of the larger daily newspapers editorialized against approving the constitution, many smaller papers came out for it. So did the the AFL-CIO, pleased that Right-to-Work was not included. The NAACP endorsed it for its strong antidiscrimination provisions. Four Catholic bishops and the Catholic press approved of removing the old constitution's prohibition against public aid to private schools. Other features of the document secured the endorsement of organizations representing the state's assessors (homestead exemption), district attorneys (original criminal jurisdiction) and municipalities (home rule).

Opposing it were the State Chamber of Commerce, the Louisiana Manufacturers' Association, the Public Service Commission and the Ku Klux Klan.

Governor Edwards and Chairman Henry stumped for its passage. But the strongest support came from a local official and convention delegate, Jefferson Parish assessor Lawrence Chehardy, who saturated New Orleans–area airwaves with ads warning of skyrocketing property taxes if the constitution were not approved.

Though the new constitution was approved by voters in only 28 of 64 parishes, its wide margin in the New Orleans area enabled it to pass with 58 percent of the vote statewide.

The new charter was substantially shorter and less unwieldy than the old, yet by national standards remains the longest, and growing.

It was inevitable that the master politician and the independent research organization would clash over the fundamental work of crafting and adopting a new constitution. Steimel's stinging criticism of its tax provisions led Edwards to dismiss PAR's claim to objectivity and impartiality as "not human, not practical and not so."

He believed this much: "PAR is definitely not pro-Edwards. One of their prejudices is against anyone who is governor." He complained that many PAR recommendations were more academic than politically feasible.

Yet Edwards later enlisted PAR's help in solving one of the thorniest practical political problems: setting priorities for highway construction projects. The Department of Transportation and Development, a longtime nest of patronage and corruption, was responsible for some of the nation's worst roads, despite the highest gasoline taxes and deepest-bonded indebtedness for highway construction. For decades, determining which highways were built or improved had been more a function of political clout than of safety considerations or traffic flow.

Following a major recommendation from a PAR study, the Legislature had adopted the first five-year construction budget in 1968. But it turned out to be reform on paper only. Outside of legislative sessions, Governor McKeithen routinely agreed to changes urged by legislators and local politicians. By 1973, $370 million was still needed to complete the $402 million in projects adopted for the first two years of the five-year plan.

Devising a highway priority plan that could work had long been an aim of PAR Associate Director Art Thiel. A freshman state representative, Richard Baker of Baton Rouge, used PAR's research and credibility to attract media support for a far-reaching bill to depoliticize highway planning.

"The administration thought it was no threat and paid no attention," remembers Baker, even after he and Thiel and two other legislators pressed for a meeting with top highway officials.

According to Baker, after he laid out his plan for scoring every project based on road conditions, traffic count and safety concerns, a senior engineer leaned over and told him, "The governor will never go for this."

"That's not what the governor told me yesterday," said Baker, who was technically telling the truth, since the governor had not mentioned the priority bill.

"We talked for hours," said Thiel. When it became apparent that the visitors were not leaving without some resolution, he continued, "Finally, one of them said, 'Hey, we can do this.'"

The bill faced opposition in both houses, but overcame it with PAR's seal of approval, which attracted strong newspaper editorial support. The dogged persistence paid off. That year the Legislature passed the highway priority plan, which stood up well for decades as one of the most effective reforms championed by PAR.

It was a signal victory for the freshman representative, who would rise to be chairman of the House Transportation Committee before his election to Congress in 1986. "I credit PAR with ability to get the attention I couldn't get on my own," Baker said later. "Their value was that over time they could do the kind of thorough analysis and it would be credible. I could do all the number crunching I wanted and people would say that's just Baker."

Besides highways and budgeting, Art Thiel's policy passion was home rule. Few more significant changes resulted from the 1974 constitution than the principle that PAR would call the "Emancipation Proclamation for local government."

The old constitution of 1921 made local governments slaves to the Legislature by expressly limiting the powers of municipalities and parishes. It took a constitutional amendment to allow parishes to write their own local charters, which only a handful of the largest parishes had done before 1974.

The new constitution allowed local governments to do anything not directly in conflict with state law. Its adoption sparked greater interest in local charters and opened a new consulting sideline for PAR. In short order, PAR assisted the writing of charters in Alexandria, Bogalusa, Covington, Donaldsonville, Hammond, Monroe, Natchitoches, Slidell, Zachary and several parishes.

The maximum fee PAR accepted for such work was $10,000, which the *Monroe Morning World* deemed a bargain compared with a figure five times higher quoted by a professional consulting firm to the Monroe Charter Commission.

In typical fashion, PAR did not advise charter commissions on what to do so much as supply them with the questions they needed to answer. Art Thiel and Paul R. Jones II, PAR's director of local affairs, compiled a checklist of options. Did the commission want a city manager or a strong mayor? How many council members, and would they be elected at-large or from districts or both? What kind of personnel system did the commission want?

Thiel informed the police jury in West Baton Rouge Parish that it could not deny the petition of a citizens' group to call an election to choose a charter commission. Faced with the prospect of a hostile charter commission being elected, the police jury wised up and appointed one. Other police juries were dismayed to learn that they could not change a charter commission's work before it was presented to the people.

Helping local citizens form their own governments was one of Thiel's most gratifying experiences at PAR. He was impressed at how quickly the citizens, many with no experience in government, could weigh the pros and cons of alternative plans and make well-reasoned choices. "When a charter is finally proposed, commission members are good at defending their decisions," he said. "We have ended up with a nucleus of well-informed citizens."

By 1980, a majority of Louisianians lived in parishes or cities with home rule charters. "Interest in local government is one of the most important developments of this decade," noted Thiel at the time. Following three decades of reform in state government, he said, "Now there is action on the local scene."

Solving the problems of public education had long been an elusive goal, as it remains today. In 1974, Governor Edwards appointed Steimel head of a commission to propose remedies for public school problems.

"He gave me good freedom in picking people to serve with me," recalls Steimel. "And I thought I had that until I found out that he packed the commission before I appointed anyone. I said, 'You gave me a commission I can't work with.' He said, 'We'll appoint some more.'" Classic doing business with Edwards.

With an appropriation from the state, Steimel contracted with PAR to hire Emogene Pliner as the commission's research director. But after a full year's study and recommendations for a professional development program for teachers, Steimel said that Edwards "gave in to the teachers. He would not fight them."

Steimel's and Pliner's work was partially vindicated when Edwards ultimately signed into law a requirement that new teachers pass the National Teachers' Examination in order to be state certified.

Despite his differences with PAR, when Edwards ran for re-election in 1975, he could take credit for accomplishing, or making progress toward, nearly all of its recommendations on the big issues of the 1971 campaign. Steimel could not disagree: "His first term was a very good term."

The voters agreed. Edwards embarked on his re-election bid with soaring approval ratings and two bland opponents, Secretary of State Wade O. Martin Jr. and state Sen. Bob Jones, the son of Sam Jones. Thanks to the new open primary, a strong economy and his own solid record, Edwards went from three grinding elections in 1971 to one tidy 62 percent win in 1975.

The governor and PAR had settled into a mutually respectful if not close working relationship. Though Edwards had criticized PAR's idealistic approach to politics, he nonetheless urged it not to change. He would later tell PAR members at their annual meeting: "If you elect to abandon the course you have chosen for yourself, you do the public a disservice."

Indeed, it was not PAR that would change course in the 1970s, but rather the man most closely identified with it.

Ed Steimel had pushed the envelope of PAR's prohibition against lobbying and electioneering. Reining him in was a standing duty of the executive committee. Though he strained at the leash at times, Steimel recognized that PAR's long-term effectiveness rested on its reputation for fairness and impartiality. Lobbying bills and getting involved in campaigns was not its role.

But whose role was it? Steimel had preached to business leaders that they had to get involved in politics in order to realize the reforms that PAR researched and recommended. The Council for a Better Louisiana chose not to get entangled in the most sensitive labor-management issues like Right-to-Work. Businessmen earlier had organized a State Chamber of Commerce, but it did nothing, and the Louisiana Manufacturers' Association had no clout. There was little coordination among the many businesses and trade organizations lobbying the Legislature and practically none at election time.

Business interests' main competitors, on the other hand—the AFL-CIO, the Teamsters and teacher unions—backed their lobbying efforts with well-financed political campaign operations to elect their friends and beat their enemies at the polls. The labor unions' election muscle played a large role in their success at the Legislature, just as business' lack thereof cost it dearly.

In 1974, premier business lobbyist Billy Brown of Kaiser Aluminum asked Steimel and PAR to devise a plan for a politically active statewide organization to advance business issues in the Legislature. Steimel accompanied Brown and others to Colorado to visit a similar organization and wrote a report with recommendations. "I had not even thought of being a part of this thing," recalled Steimel.

But Brown and colleagues had. Through early 1975, they marshaled support among business executives, including many active PAR trustees, such as PAR President Wallace Armstrong, the Ethyl plant manager.

While Steimel's penchant for lobbying was a running concern for Armstrong as PAR chairman, that very attribute made him valuable to Armstrong as an LABI founder. "He did a very good job at PAR, but the lobbying business was in him," said Armstrong. "I knew LABI could use someone like Ed."

In September, Brown, Armstrong and two others took Steimel to lunch at the City Club and asked him to head up the Louisiana Association of Business and Industry. Steimel was intrigued but also concerned, for his own security and for PAR. For three weeks he wrestled with the decision, and even experienced a mild heart attack.

Ironically, of all the advice he sought, the soundest came from Edwin Edwards. Over lunch at the mansion ("just the two of us at the long dining room table," Steimel remembers), Edwards heard out the idea for LABI. Then he said, "If I were you, I'd take it. The reason is that if you want to win in this business, you have to get heavily involved in elections. You don't amount to anything in politics until you elect someone."

Edwards recalls what else he told Steimel about his new opportunity: "I said, 'You should do it because you have completely corrupted PAR.'" Edwards was referring to what he considered to be Steimel's overt lobbying on business issues: "You should go to work for the people who you really represent rather than continuing to corrupt PAR."

The part of the conversation Steimel remembers inspired him to take the job but also to pose a challenge to LABI organizers: "I told them, if we do this, we have to match Vic Bussie. That means we have to raise a lot of money and make LAPAC [LABI's campaign arm] a really strong force in this state. They said, 'Go for it.' They also said, 'You go raise the money.'"

After 25 years with PAR, 23 of them as its director and public face, Ed Steimel left in November 1975. Though his departure and LABI's arrival would be a test for PAR, choosing a new leader was the easy part, as it had been in 1953. "It took us about 15 seconds to decide," recalls Armstrong.

Art Thiel had been second in command since 1959, when he joined the staff as research director. The quality of PAR work had reached a new level of professionalism under his guidance. A dedicated researcher and shrewd analyst, Thiel was less the public figure and political presence than Steimel was, and that would not change. "I'm not Steimel and I won't try to be," he said.

He would even change his title. Beginning with Thiel, the position of executive director became that of president, while the elected head of membership, formerly the president, would be chairman.

Thiel's greater challenge was keeping PAR from being eclipsed by LABI's shadow. Even members of the two groups had difficulty not seeing them as connected.

Steimel himself had that problem, according to Thiel, who recalled, "Ed and I had strong disagreements over issues." He said Steimel pressed him to have PAR research business issues vital to LABI. PAR did publish a Right-to-Work study in 1976 that supported LABI's position, and it recommended overhauling the workers' compensation system, another LABI priority. But Thiel and his staff did not assign the same priority to other items on LABI's agenda. The resulting friction led Thiel to ask for a meeting of the presidents of the two groups at which both agreed that PAR would consider but not give preference to LABI's requests for research studies.

"After the dust settled, it operated quite well," says Thiel. "He [Steimel] understood that it was not good to have the two considered as one."

The ascent of LABI tested PAR's finances as well as its independence. Said Thiel, "We had to prove to business people who contributed to both that we still would be doing the kind of things we wanted. The people who were not pro-business, we had to prove to them we would not be under business' thumb."

Armstrong remembered, "It was hard to keep some people on board. . . . People do not want to spend money on two different things if they think they're doing the same things."

But differences between the two groups also posed problems for some dual members. Thiel recalls one plant manager who questioned how his company could support both groups when "LABI had come out with one thing and PAR with something else."

Though PAR's membership and income increased through the 1970s, the combination of a future economic downturn and LABI's high political profile ultimately would cause many dual members to choose between them, to PAR's disadvantage.

In Edwards' second term, PAR increasingly focused on the gap between the administration's promises and claims of good government and what it actually delivered. The period produced some of PAR's best work at revealing reforms gone awry.

Edwards had promised and the new constitution mandated government reorganization. A PAR study concluded that the administration's plan more resembled regrouping of agencies and giving the governor more, not less, control. A 1978 *PAR Analysis* noted that while 256 agencies, authorities, boards and commissions had been consolidated into twenty large departments, the number of direct appointments by the governor only decreased from 1,424 to 1,340.

The most critical appointments were the top managers of the executive departments. The Legislature started off appropriately with a law to allow department heads to appoint the top officials beneath them. To no avail, PAR warned against a 1977 revision granting the governor the authority to name all undersecretaries and assistant secretaries beneath department heads.

What PAR called unsound management practices the governor deemed good self-serving politics, and he signed the bill.

In 1973, PAR had applauded a major expansion of the state's vocational-technical system, one of the group's earliest recommendations. But five years and $100 million later, PAR concluded that the enlarged network of vo-tech schools incorporated some of the worst flaws of the old system.

Politics and the influence of labor unions, rather than workforce development, guided the placement of training programs. PAR noted that courses in construction trades were located mostly in smaller towns instead of in Shreveport, Monroe and Lake Charles, where the labor unions ran their own apprenticeship programs.

A *PAR Analysis* found that businesses had 20,000 to 30,000 construction trade positions that apprenticeships were not filling. But AFL-CIO Vice-President Gordon Flory said PAR was trying to "stockpile skills" as a way to force down wages.

PAR also recognized that the vo-tech schools were pawns in a new turf battle between the elected superintendent of education and the newly created Board of Elementary and Secondary Education, which was also elected. PAR's solution was to appoint the superintendent, an idea Edwards dismissed as politically impossible, but which the Legislature adopted in 1985.

PAR also urged that vo-tech schools be placed under their own management board, which the Legislature and the governor finally created twenty years later.

Though a leading champion of public education earlier, during the integration crisis, Steimel grew disillusioned after Edwards shelved most of the recommendations of the education task force he had headed. In a 1975 speech he questioned whether his own defense of public schools in the 1960s was worth it: "I'm not sure public education in its present form can be saved. I'm not sure it should be, for its resistance to change and its intolerance of outside influences is unbelievably high."

And he added, "Just who is in charge of ignorance in Louisiana?"

Apparently some of the same people in charge of the politics. A *PAR Analysis* used a perfect example of the abuses of teacher sabbatical leave for rest and recuperation. Without giving names, it stated that a school principal who was also a state senator (whom the press identified as Gaston Gerald of Baker) had taken a medical sabbatical and was drawing a $14,000 school salary while attending the 1979 legislative session.

A year later, Gerald left both the Legislature and his school to serve a prison sentence for attempted bribery. It took twenty years to put an end to Louisiana's distinction as the only state to grant teachers rest and recuperation sabbaticals.

After Edwards' re-election, Louisiana became one of the last states in the Union to enact a campaign finance disclosure law (a 1975 version had been struck down in court). But the post-Watergate election reform wave barely lapped up on Louisiana's shores. PAR noted that the new law contained as many loopholes as limits, mainly owing to sky-high thresholds for reporting donations: $1,000 for governor and $500 for the Legislature. The study also pointed out that contributors could evade the disclosure thresholds by buying tickets to fundraisers over a period of time. And there were no limits on the numbers of contributions.

Another half-done reform involved the long-standing abusive practice of dual officeholding. Prodded by PAR since the 1960s, the Legislature had eliminated some of the more flagrant examples of "double-dipping" by politicians who held both state and local offices. Yet a 1974 *PAR Analysis* revealed that a legislator sat on the State Board of Education and that police jurors and mayors commonly served as school board members. The law also allowed legislators to serve on the State Mineral Board and the LSU Board of Supervisors.

Though the new constitution generally prohibited dual officeholding, as with gambling, the Legislature was empowered to define it. Between loopholes approved by the Legislature and narrow interpretations of the law by attorney general opinions, PAR concluded, "The very intent of the separation-of-powers doctrine, to prevent the dangerous accumulation of power in the same individuals, is subverted." Similarly, PAR was concerned that the governor's ability to appoint legislators to significant boards and commissions compromised their independence and enhanced his power.

Toward the end of Edwards' second term, he and the Legislature heeded some of PAR's calls to place in the constitution a comprehensive ban on dual officeholding. They also tightened up on bidding, purchasing and hiring practices, which would serve to curb some of the powers of the governor. The next governor, that is.

Edwards had more scrapes with grand juries, including a federal panel investigating his relationship with Korean businessman Tongsun Park. Edwards explained to reporters that he received nothing, but that Park did give his wife Elaine $10,000 to buy gifts for herself and her daughters. When asked what his wife did with the money, he deadpanned, "My daughters are trying to find that out now."

Edwards avoided the sad second-term fate of John McKeithen by not launching any massive, controversial projects, such as the Superdome, that would drain his political strength and popularity. Indeed, Edwards did not use his second term to make a lasting mark to be remembered for. There would be time for that, for he seemed to have no intention of letting his second term be his last.

The complexities of governing: Earl Long raised taxes, abolished civil service and allegedly took payoffs from organized crime; yet he borrowed least of any modern governor, built needed charity hospitals and trade schools and equalized salaries for black and white schoolteachers.

Gov. Earl Long, enraged when a PAR analysis of state revenues led to the defeat of his 1956 tax package, mistook the new Legislative Council for PAR and vetoed its appropriation.

Earl Long works the floor of the Senate in 1951.
Photo by Ken Armstrong

Key reforms initiated by Gov. Sam Jones were abolished when Earl Long beat him in 1948.
Courtesy of The Advocate

Gov. Robert Kennon restored civil service and signed the first Right-to-Work law, but it was repealed when Earl Long returned to power in 1956.
Courtesy The Advocate

Gov. Jimmie Davis was generally cooperative but resented PAR's opposition to his efforts to maintain segregation.
Courtesy The Advocate

New Orleans business leader Edgar B. Stern first voiced the need for an independent research organization.

Dr. Robert French took leave from Tulane to be the first director of PAR.

PAR's first president, Hugh Coughlin, rallied businessmen to back the fledgling organization. He tapped Ed Steimel to succeed French.

Lumberman Parrish Fuller turned down entreaties to run for governor, but was instrumental in forming PAR and was its sixth president.

John McKeithen used PAR recommendations in his campaign platform, and later signed into law the first state Code of Ethics.
Courtesy The Advocate

Gov. John McKeithen was a visionary builder and promoter but was less interested in constitutional reform.
Courtesy The Advocate

New Orleans Mayor Chep Morrison campaigned on a reform agenda but lost three governor's races.
Courtesy The Advocate

In 1967, PAR president Clifford Strauss rejected Gov. John McKeithen's demand to see PAR publications in advance.

1957 PAR President Joe D. Smith, a newspaper publisher, understood the strong symbiotic relationship between the research organization and the press.

Lester Kabacoff worked behind the scenes with Edgar Stern to generate early interest in forming PAR.

The Legislature so respected Emogene Pliner's budget research that for years it used PAR's revenue figures instead of the administration's.

AFL-CIO President Victor Bussie worked closely with PAR in supporting public education. They later parted company on labor-management issues and reapportionment.
Courtesy The Advocate

U.S. District Judge E. Gordon West appointed Ed Steimel the special master to reapportion the Louisiana Legislature in 1971.
Courtesy The Advocate

Leander Perez led demonstrators to the Capitol to pressure Gov. Jimmy Davis and legislators to defy federal desegregation orders.
Courtesy The Advocate

Archbishop Joseph Rummel excommunicated Leander Perez for defying integration. Both were PAR members.
Courtesy The Advocate

Inauguration Day 1972: Both John McKeithen and Edwin Edwards adopted key PAR recommendations in their first terms, but the group later criticized their tax and spending programs.
Photo by Carlos Harkness

Edwards on the campaign trail in 1983.
Photo by J. F. Cado

Gov. Edwin Edwards accused PAR leader Ed Steimel of trying to defeat passage of the 1974 constitution.
Courtesy The Advocate

Ed Steimel was the driving force behind PAR for 23 years, though governors complained that he frequently ignored his own bylaws that prohibited lobbying.

The PAR staff discusses a research project in 1980. From left: Art Thiel, Deidre Cruse, Emogene Pliner, Suzette DuBois and Ty Keller.

Gov. Dave Treen struggled to advance reform, but he was foiled by Edwards' legislative allies and his own political shortcomings.
Courtesy The Advocate

Wallace Armstrong was president of PAR in 1976 when he asked Ed Steimel to help form the Louisiana Association of Business & Industry.

As PAR's research director, Art Thiel accepted Gov. John McKeithen's challenge to reorganize the state budget office. He took over PAR after Steimel.

Gov. Buddy Roemer signed a stronger campaign finance reform law than PAR recommended, but his watered-down fiscal reform package was rejected by the voters.
Courtesy The Advocate

Mark Drennen went from being the first Legislative Fiscal Officer to president of PAR to state commissioner of administration.
Courtesy The Advocate

Jackie Ducote developed education policy for LABI before returning to PAR as president after Drennen.
Courtesy The Advocate

PAR praised Gov. Mike Foster's education and ethics reforms, but clashed with him over highway projects he favored on U.S. 90.

Photo by James Terry III

Chairman in 1999–2000, Jay Handelman helped guide PAR through its leadership transition.

Named president in 1999, Jim Brandt helped to redefine PAR's mission and to raise its profile.

4

Reckoning for Reform

Many PAR members and business leaders could excuse Edwin Edwards for backsliding on the reform achievements he claimed in his 1975 re-election campaign. Though his administration and its legislative allies blunted or subverted the promised progress in the areas of government reorganization, vo-tech schools, campaign finance, higher education and the public retirement system, the governor more than made up for all of the above, for the business community anyway, by signing the Right-to-Work bill, despite organized labor's pleas that he veto it.

Though the size of state government expanded rapidly during Edwards' eight years in office, so did state revenues, largely fueled by the booming oil and gas economy, thus obviating the need for tax increases.

Though more investigations and hints of scandal followed Edwards in his second term, none caught up with him. The suggestions of impropriety seemed only to enhance his stature and mystique among ordinary voters. But for the constitutional prohibition, a third successive term would have been his for the asking.

Instead, conservatives looked forward to the 1979 election as an opportunity to renew the reform agenda by combining good government with a good economy.

A strong field entered the governor's race, the first open-seat race to be run under the open primary system. When the law was passed, it was seen as the final death knell for the Republican Party. No longer would a Democrat have to battle through two costly and tiring primaries only to meet a fresh, well-heeled Republican opponent in the general election. With Republican registration under 2 percent, it seemed certain that most major contests would come down to two Democrats in a single runoff.

But the law had the opposite effect by allowing conservatives who were registered Democrats in name only to switch to the Republican Party and still participate in all elections.

The law would have another early effect. The Republicans, still few and disciplined enough to unite behind a single candidate, backed Congressman Dave Treen, who had received 43 percent of the vote against Edwards in 1972. The Democrats, who had no real party structure and less discipline, saw their numbers split by five strong contenders, all elected officeholders with substantial regional bases.

Treen wasted no time, running his first television ad in February before the October election. Polls showed him leading the whole way with Lt. Gov. Jimmie Fitzmorris in solid second place and the rest of the field split. Speaker of the House Bubba Henry and state Sen. Edgar Mouton impressed many as the most capable and intelligent of the field, but neither could build broad appeal outside their home parishes. The surprise candidate who connected most easily with rural voters, north and south, was state Sen. Paul Hardy, a dynamic campaigner from Acadiana who reminded many of Edwin Edwards.

With Treen on the right and four Democrats running in the middle, the Democrat who came closest to embracing the populist politics of Edwards and the Longs was Public Service Commissioner Louis Lambert of Ascension Parish. From his River and Florida parishes base, including Baton Rouge, he attracted strong support from black leaders and organized labor.

On election night, Treen ran below expectations but still led the field with 23 percent of the vote. Fitzmorris led in New Orleans and Jefferson, but ran poorly in most of the rest of the state. In the closing week of the primary campaign, Lambert outspent his Democratic rivals, organized the best get-out-the-vote effort in his base and squeezed past Fitzmorris into the runoff by 2,506 votes.

The open primary and the split Democratic field resulted in the lone Republican making the runoff against the most liberal and thus beatable Democrat.

Lambert had other problems. Fitzmorris filed a lawsuit challenging the election results, which kept Lambert in court and off balance through the first half of the runoff. The allegations of election irregularities, though unproven, cast a dark shadow on the public service commissioner, who trailed Treen in polls by fifteen points going into the last two weeks. Making things worse, each of the eliminated Democratic candidates came forward one by one to endorse the Republican.

Though all parties claimed no deals were made, all the endorsers would receive help from Treen supporters in retiring their campaign debts. And all would receive prominent, high-paid jobs in the Treen administration, an act that would haunt them, and him, for the rest of their political careers.

Edwin Edwards stayed out of the primary and the runoff until the final week, when he made a whirlwind campaign tour for Lambert. Again, Treen's poll lead shrank on election night to a thin margin, which Lambert came within 9,557 votes of erasing.

Republicans and businessmen were ecstatic over Dave Treen's victory, and PAR members had good reason to believe they could work with a governor whose whole career, philosophy and personality were rooted in the concept of less government more efficiently run.

Conservatives had a long agenda deferred or denied by the last Edwards years. The business sector was anxious to change the system of workers' compensation and unemployment compensation, a priority shared by PAR. In a preinauguration report, the group listed twenty recommendations in six broad areas, from "Appoint State Superintendent of Education" to "Stop Public Retirement Rip-offs."

One reform-in-name-only that needed much more work was campaign finance disclosure. A *PAR Analysis* entitled "Great Louisiana Campaign Spendathon" showed that not only was the 1979 governor's race the most expensive in America, but highest-in-the-nation reporting thresholds concealed the sources of 80 percent of the $20 million raised. A contributor could donate $1,000 in each of three reporting periods, $3,000 total, without having his name show up on a single report.

Dave Treen said and promised all the right things, but his first actions, or inactions, troubled PAR leaders accustomed to working with strong governors, which Treen was not.

On the most basic organizational level, Treen had a hard time getting things done, even making up his mind. He would exact great detail from his staff on small points, like the format of letters, but would let go unattended the appointments to critical boards, leaving many Edwards cronies in influential positions for months into the new administration. His two closest aides and longtime personal friends, John Cade and Billy Nungesser, often worked at cross purposes with each other, causing many initiatives to go awry or to remain grounded.

PAR President Art Thiel saw this firsthand in his group's attempt to set up lines of communication with the governor's office. Past chairman Wallace Armstrong, the manager of Ethyl in Baton Rouge, was to be PAR's emissary to meet with Treen each week and pursue PAR recommendations. As Thiel recalled, "Wallace would meet with Treen and talk about recommendations and what was to be done and how it was to be accomplished. And the next Friday they would meet and talk about the same thing, and the next Friday again. After a while, it became pretty obvious."

The Treen administration was not through its first legislative session when Thiel first went public with his concerns. "No one expected an overnight change in state government, but there is lack of leadership in the governor's office," he said in a speech. "The campaign promises of November are not translating to reality in June."

The *Baton Rouge Morning Advocate* scolded PAR for jumping on Treen too early. "Every administration deserves a honeymoon," stated its editorial. "It's much too early to begin looking for the nearest divorce court."

But Treen's first budget justified Thiel's early concerns. Its analysis showed that the new administration spent more freely than the previous one, starting with the $515 million surplus left over from Edwards' last year. Treen raised schoolteacher salaries, but he also increased the ranks of state employees, though Louisiana already had among the most in the nation per capita. As with Democratic administrations before it, concluded PAR, this one was spending money without an eye to the future.

Treen did please conservatives by cutting personal income taxes by $100 million, but the state's financial crisis forced him to take back the reduction three years later.

On another key tax issue, there was no point in objecting when the governor supported an increase in the homestead exemption to cover the first $75,000 of home value. During the campaign, Treen had little choice but to match runoff opponent Louis Lambert's promise to raise the exemption.

Near the end of the 1980 session, PAR noted, "It's been a session of superlatives. The Legislature introduced a record number of bills and is spending a record amount of money. Unfortunately, neither legislators nor the governor is setting records for governmental reform."

Governor Treen fired back a three-page letter challenging PAR's accuracy and stating, "PAR must have gone to sleep for five months and woke up just in time to make the charge that the Treen administration has not accomplished much." For accomplishments, he cited a teacher improvement plan, later scuttled, and an increase in per-student support to public schools.

PAR did strongly back the two major Treen education initiatives: the end of lifetime certification for teachers and the Professional Improvement Program (PIP), which was the brainchild of LABI's Ed Steimel.

The original bill linked a teacher pay increase to mandatory college courses, which would form part of recertification requirements every five years. But late in the process, the bill got away from the administration when teacher allies attached amendments to make participation optional and to lower the course minimum to three college credits to qualify for extra pay. As enacted, PIP was, according to PAR, a "$52 million giveaway." It would balloon to $92 million before it was phased out in 1989.

One Treen education reform that did stick was putting an end to staggered terms for local school boards by requiring all members to run at the same time. For two decades, PAR had been calling attention to the political game played by school boards, wherein a majority of members not up for re-election in a given cycle could cover on tough votes for those who were, knowing the favor would be returned.

Despite this needed reform, in the research organization's overall view, Treen's conservative administration continued to fall short of promise. In 1981, PAR released a report entitled "The Rise and Fall of Reorganization." It noted that the number of state agencies, though consolidated into 20 departments, had grown to 325 and that the number of direct appointments by the governor had swelled to 1,556. Treen's contribution, it stated, was to add an unnecessary, duplicative oversight committee to an effort aimed at eliminating duplication.

Treen's answer to reorganization was to create the Cost Control Commission, to be chaired by Wallace Armstrong. "We developed a very excellent report on ways we could save money and get things done for the good of everybody," said Armstrong, "but it was very much like other attempts to cut the cost of government. It was a disappointment. There was quite a gap between what needed to be done and what was going to be done."

Armstrong did not fault Treen. "He could only get done what he could get done," he said. "Inertia is a hard thing to overcome."

Art Thiel was less understanding: "I told him if he's not going to follow up and do something about it, there is no point in having a commission. He said he would do something. And next time he said it again. You know the story, there was not much done."

To PAR, reorganization was about more than tidy administration. Though the state was awash in windfalls from the federal deregulation of oil and gas prices, PAR foresaw dark clouds behind the silver lining as the national recession worsened, rising oil prices leveled off and declining production in Louisiana steepened.

The titles of PAR reports on state finances during the period demonstrate how well its words were heeded:
— May 1979: "State Budget: Eureka!"
— September 1980: "State Finance: Boom or Bust?"
— May 1981: "Riches, But Who's Embarrassed?"
— May 1982: "The Predicted Slowdown Is Here"
— September 1982: "Options for Averting a State Financial Crisis"
— December 1982: "Financial Problems: How Much, How Long?"

As budget surpluses disappeared and the governor began ordering spending and hiring freezes, PAR warned that the most conservative administration in 30 years was ignoring the opportunity to finally put the state on firm fiscal ground. Thiel's personal frustration with Treen boiled over into a scathing *Analysis* simply entitled, "Governor's Slush Fund." It lumped the Treen administration with Edwards' for using the "governor's discretionary public improvements fund" to circumvent the capital outlay process. With the $179 million spent over ten years, PAR noted, Treen for his share had granted the construction of locally requested flood control and drainage projects, boat launches, theater renovations, rodeo stands and a parking lot for a ballpark.

The state's growing budget problems also made it unlikely that the administration and Legislature would confront what PAR called "Public Retirement: Smouldering Issues." Ten years earlier, PAR had begun warning that the Legislature was not funding public retirement systems adequately to pay for the generous benefits it continued to expand, including early retirement, credit for unused sick leave and special treatment for part-time elected officials, especially legislators. As much research as PAR invested in retirement issues, their complexities and the fact that those most interested were people in the system made it difficult to start a groundswell for change. Though Treen signed into law some improvements, reform in this area would be painstaking and a long time in coming. It was not until 1995 that the Legislature barred legislators—future legislators, that is—from joining public retirement systems.

One area of reform where Treen went one better than PAR was the emerging issue of the environment. You would not know that stronger environmental regulation was a major public issue in the 1970s and '80s from reading PAR reports. Aside from a 1982 review of the state's air quality program, which PAR pronounced "in fairly good shape," the organization paid little attention to the issue that was stirring greater controversy and awareness in the press and the public. Critics would link PAR's lack of interest in state environmental regulation to the dominance of industrial companies among its dues-paying members.

One major reform never listed among PAR's recommendations was taking environmental regulation out of the Department of Natural Resources and establishing the cabinet-level Department of Environmental Quality, a significant change that Treen signed into law in 1983.

Overall, though, the reform record of the Treen administration was mixed, owing not only to the governor's own limitations but also to the resistance of a band of influential legislators. Treen's policy proposals fared better in the House, where he had a strong ally in Speaker John Hainkel. But the initiatives often failed in the Senate, which came to be known as the "graveyard of reform." A new antiadministration power base had formed in the upper chamber, which, under the new constitution, had elected its first president, Michael O'Keefe of New Orleans. The soft-spoken, unfailingly courteous O'Keefe maneuvered expertly behind the scenes to subvert good-government measures he would publicly endorse. It earned him the nickname "the Spider."

While the administration was no match for O'Keefe, the U.S. Attorney's office was. But even after O'Keefe was convicted in a financial fraud scheme in 1981, other senators, led by new President Sammy Nunez of Chalmette, filled the void of power left open by the governor.

Treen had a bigger political problem outside the Capitol, for Edwin Edwards had begun running for governor again from the day he left office. It frustrated more than puzzled Treen admirers that their candidate maintained high public approval ratings, with sky-high marks for integrity and trust, and yet he consistently trailed Edwards by 15–20 points in gubernatorial trial heats. Many of Edwards' allies in the Legislature, indeed many still entrenched in the state bureaucracy, felt encouraged to fend off or ignore changes that Treen wanted while they waited for Edwards to return.

He did, with a vengeance.

"Where has it gone? Where has all the money gone?" candidate Edwards would cry out again and again on the 1983 campaign trail. He referred, of course, to the $500 million surplus he left to Treen in 1980. Treen and the Legislature had spent it all and more after giving some back to taxpayers, only to be caught short in the oil bust and economic downturn that occurred midway through his term.

Fiscal responsibility: of all things for Edwin Edwards to beat up Dave Treen on. It worked, not just because the numbers were indisputable (whether or not Treen was entirely to blame) but also because voters believed, or desperately wanted to believe, that Edwards could make good economic times roll again.

Thanks to a campaign finance law laden with loopholes and still without a limit on contributions or loans, Edwards amassed a $12 million war chest double that of the incumbent, pro-business Republican governor.

Still, Edwards had minefields to navigate. He caught his best break in the summer when the Republican U.S. attorney in Baton Rouge, after a long investigation of a pension benefits plan aimed at state employees, issued a report that criticized Edwards' role but did not seek indictments.

But a tragic personal loss for Edwards may have sealed his election victory. The one issue that tested well for Dave Treen was the few pardons and paroles he granted compared with Edwards' far more liberal policy, with a fair share of documented abuses. With polls showing Treen beginning to close the gap, the campaign readied a hard-hitting commercial blasting Edwards for letting career criminals go free and commit more crimes.

But before the spot aired, Edwards' younger brother Nolan was gunned down in his Crowley law office by a former client whom Edwards had pardoned years before. The death devastated Edwards, who withdrew from campaigning for a week after the funeral. But also hard hit was the Treen campaign, which out of respect and good sense shelved the pardon commercial.

Edwards' campaign bounced back stronger than did Treen's, bereft of its most explosive issue. It wasn't a race after that. Edwards' crowds grew in number and enthusiasm as he raised the ante of his message to messianic proportion. "The healer is coming," he told a Ville Platte audience. "Someone is coming to deliver you from your despair."

By election night, only the challenger's vote count was in question. Edwards rolled up a gubernatorial record of just over one million votes as he trounced the respected, scandal-free incumbent 62–36 percent with a few votes scattered among seven also-rans.

The remarkable comeback (if he ever left) marked the high point of Edwin Edwards' fabled career, for though he would be elected governor again, with even more votes, he would experience more lows than highs in the rest of his public life.

Edwards started his third term with PAR's rare support for a tax hike. PAR endorsed the administration's proposed doubling of the gasoline tax dedicated to highway construction and maintenance. But three months later, the research group would decry a Senate bill to take $200 million of the gasoline tax money to fund highway and drainage projects outside of the priority system Art Thiel had helped to create. "Politics based on something for nothing," scolded a *PAR Bulletin*. The bill was defeated, but the gasoline tax increase would be the last major proposal of Edwards' third term that PAR would back.

During the Treen administration, when he and the Legislature did not heed warnings to rein in spending, PAR had predicted that the next governor and Legislature would be forced to raise taxes. But when Edwards unveiled a $1.2 billion tax package in the special session, conservatives howled, while PAR responded, once again, that the state should cut its number of employees, which ranked Louisiana ninth in the nation per capita. Legislators approved more than half the package before revolting and killing the rest of the taxes. Edwards concluded that half a loaf was worse than none, because the tax issue would have to be faced again if the state were to maintain the level of services to which the people had become accustomed.

Thiel stated in a newspaper interview that he always heard the same answer to why Louisiana taxes and spends more: because we are different. After 25 years of working for reform in Louisiana, Thiel could only respond, "Maybe it's time we stopped being different."

In that spirit, PAR advanced one of its boldest recommendations in the spring of 1984 when it called for the repeal of the homestead exemption.

But Louisiana was not ready to stop being that different, as most Louisiana politicians ignored PAR's call, except for those who criticized it. The East Baton Rouge Parish assessor pointed out that the constitutional amendment to raise the exemption to $75,000 was approved by 90 percent of voters.

The disappointments were not over. Edwards and the more liberal Legislature elected with him easily rolled back the reforms Treen had labored to pass. After PAR and LABI finally made the case in 1983 to replace a litigation-driven workers' compensation system with administrative process with a uniform schedule of benefits, Edwards signed a law in 1984 to abolish the new program.

Analyzing the 1984 special and regular sessions in which taxes and spending were increased along with yet more unfunded retirement benefits, Thiel said, "We seem to be regressing after years of reform," and concluded, "It would be better if they never came to the Capitol."

The voters seemed to agree, for that fall they rejected all five constitutional amendments put before them, including a corporate tax hike that the Legislature had already appropriated the money from.

For Thiel, that session and a quarter of a century at PAR would be enough, as he announced his retirement in June 1984. In his retirement speech in November, he said of Edwin Edwards, "He has the ability. But does he have the willingness? Does he have the desire?"

He may have, but uppermost on Edwards' mind was a federal grand jury in New Orleans that was about to return indictments against him and six others in a hospital deal. He would survive two trials (a mistrial and an acquittal), but the ordeal, combined with the depressed economy and state budget crises, would turn his third term into a political and personal nightmare.

When Earl Ryan left his post as research director for the Citizens' Research Council in Michigan to become PAR's fourth director and president, two different federal grand juries were investigating the governor of Louisiana and state and federal panels were probing the World's Fair in New Orleans.

Ryan's first public statement, measured with optimism and some wishful thinking, called on the state to "elevate the debate" beyond more confrontations with the U.S. Justice Department. "I look forward to the day when discussions of pension funding and healthcare cost containment and similar issues would appear on the front page, and I would like PAR to be a credible voice in those things."

Though distracted by preparation for his fall trial, the governor together with the Legislature did bounce back from the woeful 1984 session to pass a package of education reforms. The Legislature finally adopted PAR's recommendation to change the position of superintendent of education from elective to appointive, though the real catalyst was a 1982 scandal leading to the conviction of two high-ranking officials in the department. Lawmakers also followed another longstanding PAR recommendation in eliminating tenure for principals and supervisors.

Responding to broad civic and editorial pressure, the governor and lawmakers placed in a trust fund most of the $700 million windfall from the so-called 8(g) settlement with the federal government concerning offshore oil and gas revenues. The Legislature did take $100 million off the top for the distressed 1985–86 budget, but sent $600 million, plus future income, to the trust fund, from which only three-fourths of the interest earnings would be appropriated to educational enhancement programs.

Yet legislators once again refused to require periodic teacher recertification, salary increases for those who passed the National Teacher Exam and an increase in higher education funding.

Nor did the Legislature come to grips with the mounting fiscal crisis, as it passed two straight budgets based on overly optimistic revenue estimates, which led to mid-year across-the-board cuts and year-end deficits. Off limits to cuts was the fastest-growing budget component, service on the state's swelling debt.

The major business reform of the session, repeal of the prevailing wage law, was vetoed by the governor.

Though Earl Ryan did not become a familiar public figure like past presidents Ed Steimel and Art Thiel, or even research director Emogene Pliner, he nonetheless gave PAR a new public face by overhauling the look and content of the *PAR Analysis*. The familiar 12- to 16-page in-depth studies were replaced with 6-page pamphlets with colorful graphics and magazine layouts. But there were fewer of them, only four published in 1985 and 1986.

Despite Ryan's efforts to elevate the debate, or even to change the subject, Louisiana politics focused more than ever on the legal problems of Edwards and others in his administration. After two years in Louisiana, Ryan left to take a similar position in Indiana.

The balance of Edwards' third term was marked by scandal fatigue and budget misery, as the governor and the Legislature hit an impasse over correcting mounting deficits. Freshly acquitted in early 1986, Edwards proposed a state lottery and casino gambling in New Orleans, and even included $237 million in gambling revenues in his executive budget. But legislators, distancing themselves from the now unpopular governor, shunned his gambling package and took the initiative to cut the budget when he would not. They also resorted to a "temporary" suspension of the state sales tax on food, utilities and prescription drugs, which has been renewed ever since.

It wasn't pretty. It still wasn't fiscal reform. But the 1986–87 budget did mark the first time a Legislature had rejected an Edwards spending plan and gone their own way. "We lost control of them," Edwards told reporters, blaming "media publicity about an independent Legislature."

Appropriate to the fiscal challenge facing Louisiana, PAR reached inside state government to hire Legislative Fiscal Officer Mark Drennen as its new president. It was LABI president Ed Steimel that urged Drennen to apply for the job. The New York native had worked for the Legislative Fiscal Office since its inception in 1974 (a key PAR recommendation) and had been its director since 1979.

What attracted him, said Drennen, "was the idea of running a good-government, watchdog group" but also "essentially to get out of government." In his previous position, three of the four administrations he had served under were Edwin Edwards'. "I felt we did important work, but with the administration the way they were, you were not able to get done what you wanted done, and after a while that wears on you."

Still, leaving government was a big step, and Drennen's wife Marian asked him if he would ever go back. "I told her no, not unless the right governor came along and asked me to be commissioner of administration."

In his last forecast as LFO, Drennen projected $3.5 billion in revenue, $400 million less than predicted by the governor's budget office. Once out of government, Drennen could go public with the reason for the wide gulf between the two sets of numbers. He said that Budget Officer Ralph Perlman, at Edwards' instruction, "manipulates the numbers to come up with any dollar amount they want to put in the budget."

"An absolute lie," Perlman snapped back. Yet Edwards confirmed as much during the 1983 governor's race when he laughed at a Treen aide who said the governor had no control over civil servant Perlman's budget figures. "Man, he's got you conned. When I was governor Ralph would come up with any figures I wanted him to come up with," said Edwards. He continued, "There were times Ralph didn't want to go face them [legislators], but I'd say, 'Ralph, that's what you're paid for. I don't want to go lie to them. You go lie to them.'"

Before Drennen could begin reviewing state finances, he had to reckon with PAR's own budget problems. "Nobody on the search committee knew how bad things were," he remembers. In 1987, the organization's income, predominately membership dues, totaled $534,000, down from its 1984 peak of $652,000. When that number was adjusted for inflation, the group showed barely more operating income than the 1951 total of $107,650. And it was dropping.

Downsizing in the oil patch, business mergers, relocations of corporate staff and competition from LABI, CABL and more active chambers of commerce were taking their toll. The nature of the membership was changing, too. When Earl Ryan took over in 1986, he and the executive committee decided to raise the minimum dues from $50 to $100 to cover the printing and mailing expenses of servicing each membership. But in so doing, the group lost half of its 3,000 dues-paying members, primarily individuals and small businesses that provided PAR a broader base.

Budget cuts were made somewhat easier by the imminent retirement of a number of staffers. The harder part of the job, completely new for Drennen, was membership recruitment and fundraising events, which entailed organizing ten breakfasts and lunches a year. While distracting, the business challenge gave the new president some perspective on what the state was going through.

Like Steimel and Thiel before him, Drennen warmed to public debate and invited controversy, with comments such as his unusual take on the disastrous oil bust: "I think falling oil prices are the best thing that ever happened to this state." His reasoning was that lawmakers were now forced to make hard choices they had avoided.

At this point, all other issues in state government were secondary to budget matters. Drennen devoted PAR publications in 1987 to a four-part series, "Financing Louisiana's Future." The headline of the first special report said it all: "Budget Reform Essential to Fiscal Sanity."

Just in time for the governor's race, state finance was finally moved to the front burner, and this time PAR wasn't alone in the kitchen.

The growing field of candidates for governor in 1987 were joined on the public stage by Freeport McMoRan CEO Jim Bob Moffett, whose campaign was not for office but for fiscal reform. The high-powered executive mounted and financed an extensive public relations campaign to galvanize public support for a plan to reduce spending and to balance the tax burden between business and individuals. At its core, Moffett's plan would cut the state sales tax in half and lower the homestead exemption to $25,000.

All the candidates, even Edwards, took the fiscal reform pledge, knowing, as with all campaign promises, that its fulfillment would be subject to interpretation and compromise.

Yet, another movement seemed to capture the public's attention, as expressed on bumperstickers: A.B.E.—Anyone But Edwards.

In perhaps the most high-ranking field of challengers ever, three congressmen, a former congressman and the secretary of state qualified to run against the wounded but still potent governor. Republican Congressman Bob Livingston, with his base in the New Orleans area, was installed as the early favorite to make the runoff. Congressman Billy Tauzin hoped to appeal to Edwards' disaffected Cajun base, while Secretary of State Jim Brown, the only challenger to have run and won statewide, banked on running well in North Louisiana and the cities. Speedy Long hoped his name could still rally a rural populist base, but he would not be a factor.

Least known, underfunded and written off earliest was maverick Democratic Congressman Buddy Roemer. Of the few voters who recognized his name, most thought he was his father, Charlie Roemer, who had been convicted on federal racketeering charges along with Mafia boss Carlos Marcello.

Though lashed with sky-high negative ratings in polls, Edwards still commanded the intense loyalty of black voters, whose voting strength, 27 percent of registrants, almost ensured him a spot in the runoff. The lucky candidate would be the one who would meet him there.

The polls from spring to late summer hardly budged from Edwards in the low 20s to Livingston in the high teens, followed by, in varying order, Tauzin and Brown, and, last, Roemer in single digits.

But once voters actually started listening to the candidates in September, Roemer's voice stood out as the most articulate and focused on the matter at hand, as expressed in one impromptu pledge that set his campaign on fire: "It's time to slay the dragon."

The Roemer flame spread south when the *New Orleans Times-Picayune* turned its back on hometown candidate Livingston and endorsed Roemer, who by now was attracting legions of college-educated volunteers who had never been involved in a political campaign before.

Edwards, who had based his one shot on getting the staid Republican Livingston in the runoff, knew it was over when Roemer passed the field, passed him, and led the primary 33–27 percent. Edwards withdrew from the race that night. But what some saw as the end of his career would turn into a strategic retreat, which gave Roemer the Governor's Mansion but which also denied him the consensus majority that would help him keep it.

Perhaps no governor before Roemer took office faced with more desperate financial straits or backed by a greater consensus for reform. Jim Bob Moffett and fiscal reform would have to wait until Roemer and the Legislature could stanch the flow of red ink from an accumulated three-year debt of $800 million. Roemer and his advisers conceived of a state recovery district, which floated more than $1 billion in bonds (which also financed a teacher pay raise) to be repaid by dedicating one cent of the sales tax for seven years.

Fiscal conservatives swallowed hard. "I never thought I would be in the position of getting up in front of anybody and saying the state needs to borrow money," Drennen told a PAR conference. Yet he explained that he saw no other choice to pay off the debt and to relieve the pressing cash-flow shortage.

That done, the 1988 regular session achieved a wider range of PAR-recommended reforms than any before it, including the initial sessions under John McKeithen in 1964 and Edwin Edwards in 1972. At the top of the list was a balanced budget, the first in three years, brought about by significant cuts but also some tax and fee increases.

Roemer had been the first governor to finance his campaign according to self-imposed rules stricter than the law. His campaign finance reform bill of 1988 brought Louisiana from the bottom to the top in regulating election spending, including limits on contributions and loans, full disclosure of all receipts and expenditures and a prohibition on converting surplus campaign funds to personal use.

PAR labeled Roemer's Children First Act "a giant step." It called for the replacement of lifetime teaching certificates with periodic renewals, a teacher evaluation plan, an across-the-board teacher pay raise and a cash-award school incentive plan for improvement. The governor tried but failed to limit the Minimum Foundation Program to instructional costs and to give local school districts more leeway to finance noninstructional costs.

Business setbacks under Edwards were reversed by the repeal of prevailing wage, which had increased the cost of state construction projects, and by changing workers' compensation from a judicial system to an administrative one.

The public employees' retirement systems finally were placed on a sound actuarial basis, the ethanol subsidy was repealed, tourism promotion was increased and generic drugs were approved for Medicaid recipients.

The next order of business was the long-awaited reform of the tax structure. Drennen and PAR joined with Moffett and other business leaders to formulate and sell a tax reform plan to the public. Drennen estimates he made 200 speeches on the subject to civic groups around the state.

But as the tax reform special session opened, more and more legislators were complaining about the Roemer Treatment. Though the governor was good at making speeches and talking to the press, he neglected the care and feeding of politicians—returning phone calls, keeping appointments, keeping commitments. The little things (big to those affected), which Edwin Edwards and John McKeithen on their worst days never ignored, were routinely dismissed by Roemer and aides as "old-style politics."

When Moffett, Drennen and fiscal reform allies arrived at the Capitol, they found a Legislature not softened up by the governor but hardened instead by his preachments. Even worse, they discovered Roemer himself was soft on tax reform, as he jettisoned the lowering of the homestead exemption, the core of the plan, when the Legislature resisted.

Instead, after much wrangling, Roemer and the Legislature agreed on a watered-down plan that adjusted personal and corporate income tax rates and raised business and "sin" taxes. The plan was designed to be revenue neutral but would still require $200 million in cuts to balance the budget.

An analysis commissioned by the fiscal reform group stated that the changes in the personal income tax rates would affect only families of four with incomes over $40,000. But the *PAR Analysis* calculated the break-even point to be $27,500, which would increase taxes for two-thirds of Louisiana families. The press jumped on the difference as an indication that the administration was cooking the numbers.

By its policy, PAR took no position on the single constitutional amendment, but its lukewarm *Analysis* did not identify many reasons to vote yes.

Roemer endorsed the amendment and ran ads asking for voter approval, making it a referendum of sorts on himself and his administration. But his stance provided a target for his critics, who had been looking for the opportunity to take him down a peg.

Though some black legislators backed the plan, many others, still chafing at health care and social spending cuts (and still close to Edwin Edwards), put out the word in their communities to vote no.

On the far other side of the scale, the newest member of the Legislature seized the opportunity to launch an anti-tax campaign to promote his conservative image to growing, enthusiastic audiences statewide. The Roemer tax reform plan would be the spark that would enkindle David Duke's races for the Senate and governor.

"We can't quit," Buddy Roemer would say on the night his tax reform plan failed, 55–45 percent. Yet the loss would mark a turning point in the Roemer administration, which would more retreat from reform than advance it in the rest of his term.

With the governor assuming a more low-key, supportive role, some other elements of fiscal (not tax) reform would pass in the fall, along with elimination of the $3 license tag and the transportation trust fund called TIMED.

But increasingly, PAR and the Roemer administration found themselves at odds on budget issues. In 1990, Drennen would criticize Roemer's $360 million tax package to go with "the swamp we call a state budget." He also blasted Roemer for "not being there" as senators overthrew the governor's hand-picked Senate president and as teacher allies suspended the hated teacher evaluation plan devised by the education superintendent he had appointed.

Distracted by the breakup of his marriage, Roemer seemed increasingly adrift in the final two years of his term.

Having not opposed the lottery, which passed a vote of the people in 1990, Roemer would sign the riverboat gambling bill and, after some soul searching, would also decide against vetoing the legalization of video poker. Though LABI's Ed Steimel railed against all forms of gambling, PAR would only note, as it did in the 1980s, that lotteries and casinos were not reliable revenue sources.

As for the threat of corruption, Roemer eased the concerns of gambling critics by promising to tightly regulate the new industry, beginning with the gaming board appointments he would make the first order of business after his re-election.

5

ONE FOR HISTORY

By the time Buddy Roemer saw David Duke coming, it was too late. In the summer of 1991, the governor actually bragged to a reporter that his poll numbers looked so good he could push back the start of his campaign from the Fourth of July to Labor Day.

Though the state representative and former Ku Klux Klan leader had surprised the political world by polling 43 percent against U.S. Sen. J. Bennett Johnston the year before, Roemer and many others wrote that off as an aberration, as voters sending a message to the veteran Washington Democrat.

The governor was not worried about Edwin Edwards' latest comeback bid either, seeing it, rather, as his own ticket for re-election. He even taunted his predecessor through the press. "Don't quit on me, Edwin, like you did last time."

But had the governor got out on the trail more, or listened to local politicos, he may have recognized that Duke was doing far better among voters than the poll numbers suggested. Met by enthusiastic crowds at well-staged rallies and mobbed while walking through parish festivals, the maverick candidate could brag his campaign was "flying below radar."

It eventually dawned on Roemer that he was in a far more vulnerable position than had been Senator Johnston, who only caught opposition from one side. Roemer was being savaged on one end by Duke for being a phony conservative and on the other by Edwards for failing to make government work. Edwards would cite an obvious example: "Could he at least mow the grass on the interstate?" as every head in the crowd nodded.

Roemer was falling victim to that peculiar Edwards invention, the open primary. Roemer won in 1987 by taking the hard right away from Bob Livingston, but after moving to the middle to govern, he found himself outflanked in 1991 by both Edwards and Duke.

First elected as a conservative Democrat, Roemer had reluctantly joined the Republican Party, but the two never warmed to each other. He did not even seek the party's endorsement, which went to Congressman Clyde Holloway, the favorite of the religious right.

If getting it from both ends was not enough, Roemer was blindsided in the final two weeks of the primary campaign by an independent, half-million-dollar TV ad attack from Jack Kent. The brash owner of Marine Shale, a waste recycler being run out of business by state and federal environmental regulators, took revenge on Roemer with devastatingly funny commercials that mocked his truthfulness and competence.

Kent's old friend Edwards denied any connection to the attack ads, which nonetheless worked like a charm to keep Roemer off-balance and off-message in the closing days of the campaign.

Though the last polls showed Roemer headed to a runoff with Edwards, the governor knew he was slipping badly. On election night, he and his son watched a baseball game on television as the election returns poured in with his defeat. Edwards led with 523,000 votes, 34 percent, to Duke's 491,000, 32 percent. Roemer ran a lame third at 26.5 percent, ahead of Holloway at 5 percent.

The open primary had managed to polarize the electorate to the extremes. Over 63 percent had voted Republican, a record, yet the incumbent Republican and the endorsed Republican both finished out of the money.

With the entire political world turning its shocked attention to Louisiana, the Duke surge continued two weeks more. He took the fight to Edwards, who appeared rather uneasy and unsure in a statewide televised debate. An independent poll two weeks before the runoff election showed Edwards leading only 46–42 percent, with Duke commanding a large majority among whites, 58–28 percent.

The Louisiana voter was having a hard time coming back to Edwin Edwards, but then became resigned to it, as the famous bumpersticker framed the issue:

VOTE FOR THE CROOK. IT'S IMPORTANT.

One by one, the state's newspapers endorsed Edwards, who seemed amused at their discomfort. He joked to a group of Rotarians, before they wrote him checks, that a one-armed man told him he would stay at home on election day because "I cannot hold my nose and vote for you at the same time."

Also, conservatives initially curious about Duke were beginning to learn more about him than they wanted to know, such as his recent associations with neo-Nazi groups and the virulently racist and anti-Semitic books sold at a Duke-run bookstore.

The more questions raised about Duke, the more assurances Edwards gave that his only self-interest was in leaving a legacy of good government. His fourth administration, he said, would be "one for history." He wasn't kidding.

The once-close election ended in a route, as Edwards piled up a record vote in a governor's race: 1,057,031 to Duke's 671,009, or 61–39 percent. The 79.9 percent turnout was within a hair of the record set in 1960 when Jimmie Davis beat Chep Morrison.

Shortly after his fourth inauguration, Edwards had the PAR staff and board members over to the Governor's Mansion for a party for research director Emogene Pliner, retiring after 41 years at the organization she had gone to work for after college. Edwards drew the biggest laugh, even from Ed Steimel, when he told Pliner,

"You are the first person to retire from PAR I was sorry to see go."

The transition was a grace period for Edwards, but the basic, unsolved problems that helped to cripple his third administration lay waiting for his fourth. As in 1983, on the campaign trail in 1991 Edwards had attacked the incumbent's fiscal policies without offering specific solutions. The one position he did take, calling a constitutional convention for fiscal reform, was criticized by PAR President Mark Drennen as a dodge, because the Legislature had all the power it needed to change the tax code.

As governor-elect, Edwards dismissed Drennen's notion as political fantasy: "The Legislature will never screw up the courage and face the realities facing the state and by two-thirds solve the problem."

The two-thirds majority was the key. It posed an almost insurmountable barrier for a Legislature seeking to broaden the income tax or to lower the homestead exemption. But a constitutional convention would need only a simple majority vote to send sweeping tax changes to the people.

By whatever method, it would take the full commitment of a strong governor to confront the tax issue, develop a solution and sell it to the people. To succeed, fiscal reform would have to be the primary focus of the new administration.

But another issue was ahead in line on Edwards' agenda. Throughout the campaign, he had deferred to the mayor of New Orleans on the issue of a land-based casino. But as it wound its way through the Legislature, the mayor's casino bill became the governor's. After it fell short by one vote in the House, the administration's forces surprised foes by pulling it from the calendar and passing it in a highly controversial and disputed vote. As with the riverboat and video poker legislation approved during Roemer's administration, there was no provision for a local vote of the people on the New Orleans casino.

Hostile public reaction ended Edwards' brief fourth honeymoon and sent his approval ratings back to the depths.

His diminished popularity made it ever more unlikely that he could lead the people toward making hard choices. He persisted with his idea of calling a constitutional convention for fiscal reform, but added the wrinkle of having the Legislature be the delegates. With the bar lowered from two-thirds to a simple majority, Edwards had the best opportunity of any governor yet to change the tax system.

But to what? Edwards went on record supporting sweeping tax reform, but, for specifics, he called upon PAR, CABL and others to recommend constitutional changes.

PAR went back to its basics. Cut spending. Limit debt. Prohibit using surplus funds for operational expenses. Require feasibility studies for capital outlay projects. Give the Legislature more flexibility on taxing income by taking the rates out of the constitution. Allow local governments to levy income taxes. And, of course, lower the homestead exemption to the first $25,000 of assessed value, with a circuit breaker for low-income taxpayers.

PAR also stated that the legislator convention should not raise taxes without a two-thirds vote and that the whole document should go to the people.

CABL and others presented more general recommendations.

Then they waited on the governor, who said he was drafting his own plan. Finally, he said, he would release it when he addressed the opening of the convention. That's too late, stated Drennen, for it left no time to educate the public and build their support, without which no group of legislators would venture far.

When the legislators did meet in a postsession convention, Edwards surprised longstanding critics by calling for strong fiscal and tax reform. But then, after giving his speech, he removed himself from the convention and left it to founder. When called upon to get involved, he shot back, "That's what they criticized me for for twenty years. Where is all this good-government, independent Legislature business?"

The convention did labor to write one proposal that included some spending and debt reforms but left tax policy untouched. The people rejected the proposal anyway, along with all five constitutional amendments on the ballot, as a general sign of contempt for the political leadership.

PAR had offered no new recommendations, but since they had never been tried, they were hardly old. The governor's response was. Faced with the running budget crisis, he reverted to across-the-board midyear spending cuts, which, because the majority of revenues are dedicated, fell most heavily on higher education. He told the Legislature it had little choice but to raise the state sales tax to five cents to cover state operations in 1993–94.

As Edwards had experienced in his third term, the more money he needed from the Legislature, the less influence he had over it. Midway through his last term, he remarked that he "lost control of them" again when a new coalition of conservative and moderate lawmakers began making informed, selective reductions in the executive budget, especially in mushrooming Medicaid programs.

The expansion of gambling dominated the headlines in 1993, from Harrah's winning the license to operate the New Orleans casino, to the explosion of video poker truckstops, to the riverboat commission handing out casino licenses to firms connected to friends of the governor and key legislators.

Gov. Buddy Roemer's attempt to control riverboat gambling by limiting the number of licenses to fifteen worked to create a lucrative market for friends of Edwards and legislative leaders. In 1999, the U.S. Justice Department would indict Edwards, his son Stephen, state Sen. Greg Tarver and four others in a conspiracy to rig the awarding of the licenses.

Though gambling controversies held center stage, 1993 was also the year many long-awaited fiscal reforms became law. For years, PAR had been beating the drum on the need to restrict state debt. Still, it was hard to get the focus of legislators, not to mention the public, until debt service started eating a growing hole in the state operating budget.

By 1992, 12 percent of the state general fund budget was going to pay debt service, triple the percentage of ten years before. Adding to the problem, the Edwards administration ran up the state credit card even more that year with its pork-laden capital outlay bill, which was widely regarded as payback for casino votes.

In 1993, state Rep. Sean Reilly proposed a constitutional amendment to put an effective $200-million-per-year limit on general bonded indebtedness. The measure was designed to quickly reduce debt service, thus freeing up money to be used on services instead of interest. The amendment attracted such attention and support that the leadership, in order to stay ahead of the House, was forced to embrace it.

That fall, voters approved debt limitation, feasibility studies for capital outlay projects and a requirement that surpluses and other one-time money be used only for debt reduction. Along with constitutional requirements for balanced budgets and the Revenue Estimating Conference, the work of fiscal reform was largely accomplished, leaving the tougher nut of tax reform to crack.

PAR members could be hopeful that another assault on the homestead exemption was no farther away than the election of a strong business governor.

In 1994, newlywed Edwards announced that he would not seek a fifth term the following year. An era was ending, and so too was his time in the public spotlight, or so he thought.

The last legislative session under Governor Edwards had adjourned and the governor's race was just picking up steam when that perennial force in Louisiana politics weighed in, as FBI agents armed with search warrants fanned out across the state.

Government wiretaps had picked up conversations of video poker truckstop operators discussing payments to state legislators for their help in killing bills that would allow parishes to vote on banning gambling. In an unusual, controversial move, the U.S. attorney in Baton Rouge released the search warrant affidavit that contained wiretapped transcripts of the alleged conspirators freely dropping the names of powerful legislators they sought to influence. The transcripts were sensational reading that reminded the citizenry that more than tax reform and term limits belonged atop the state's agenda.

A year later, state Sen. Larry Bankston and the Dean of the Senate, B. B. "Sixty" Rayburn, would be charged with racketeering and conspiracy along with the owners of a major video poker business. Most legislators mentioned on the tapes were not charged, but the damage was done, as a number of senior lawmakers, including Rayburn and Senate President Sammy Nunez, were defeated while others chose not to run again.

In 1997, Rayburn would be acquitted at trial, but Bankston was convicted on a lesser count and sent to prison for three years. That trial was not over before the even more serious riverboat corruption investigation of Edwin Edwards, his son Stephen and others came to light.

To PAR, the infusion of gambling money into politics only highlighted the lax ethical laws that made the corruption of lawmakers all the easier if not inevitable. That summer, in their first joint endeavor, PAR and the Bureau of Governmental Research in New Orleans launched an in-depth analysis of how to strengthen state ethics laws.

The federal investigation threw gasoline on smoldering antigambling sentiments, sending candidates scrambling to stake out safe positions from local option to all-out repeal.

The 1995 election was only the second in 24 years in which Edwin Edwards was not on the ballot. Making his comeback bid, former governor Buddy Roemer was determined to take back the right from David Duke, also running again. Again, the Republicans endorsed a little-known lawmaker, this time state Rep. Quentin Dastugue of Metairie.

State Treasurer Mary Landrieu and Lt. Gov. Melinda Schwegmann, both of New Orleans, and Congressman Cleo Fields of

Baton Rouge vied for the Democratic votes that had long formed Edwards' base.

Filling out the wide field was state Rep. Robert Adley and attorney Phil Preis, who was spending his own money on an aggressive outsider campaign. Also writing his own checks, though few could figure why, was conservative Democratic state Sen. Mike Foster of Franklin.

Instead of announcing his candidacy on the Capitol steps, Roemer stood in front of the barbed-wire fence of the parish prison. He ran television commercials advocating the return to chain gangs. In a prep session with his staff, when asked where he stood on the death penalty, he winked and said, "Right next to the switch."

The voters didn't buy it. Roemer started well ahead of the pack, but polls showed his support was very soft. A large number of identified conservatives remained undecided, which encouraged Duke's claim of once again flying beneath radar.

The polls showed Landrieu running right behind Roemer, but unable to shake off Schwegmann and the rest of the pack.

Just before qualifying opened, the shakeup on the right began when Dastugue, unable to raise money despite the GOP endorsement, dropped out and backed Roemer.

But the big story was that David Duke was not attracting the same crowds, excitement or money as in his first two statewide campaigns. His political stock reduced to that of a spoiler, Duke was looking to get out of the race, but not without profiting from it. Unknown to the public at the time, he and Mike Foster met in the coffeeshop of the Monteleone Hotel in New Orleans, where Duke said he might not run and offered to sell his mailing list for $100,000.

Foster agreed and funneled a personal check through an employee's company to a mailing list outfit, which turned the cash over to Duke. Foster omitted the payment from his campaign finance report because he did not use the list and, as he would say,

"It ain't cool to put out there that you bought something from David Duke." The voters would not know about the incident for four more years.

A week before qualifying opened, Duke announced he was pulling out of the race. That created a vacuum on the anti-Roemer right, which Mike Foster promptly filled by switching to the Republican Party on the day he qualified. Foster's hard-line pro-gun, anti-gambling positions and his tractor-driving, spot-welding commercials struck a chord among rural conservatives that the reinvented Roemer did not.

In short order, Foster's campaign began to move from his base in southwest Louisiana to rural North Louisiana and finally to the suburbs and the cities. Again, Roemer could feel the gap closing on him.

As Schwegmann faded in the stretch, Mary Landrieu needed only to win over enough black votes to secure her spot in the runoff. When a top supporter, a black minister, issued a statement through her campaign that blacks needed to back Landrieu as the only viable Democrat, Cleo Fields angrily accused the state treasurer of racist politics. The two ended the primary trading the charge that the other was playing the race card.

In a broad field, the open primary develops into two single-shot primaries in one, as liberal and conservative voters go their separate ways. Usually, the polarization causes the strongest candidates from the left and the right to emerge.

In the final week of the primary, Foster left Roemer in the dust and ran first. Landrieu seemed to be holding on to second place, until a late tide of rural black votes pushed Fields barely ahead. By a margin of 1,400 votes over third-place finisher Landrieu, Cleo Fields became the first African American in the Twentieth Century to win a spot in a statewide runoff.

True to form, the open primary favored the most conservative and most liberal candidates. Though Fields ran a passionate runoff campaign, Foster glided to a 64–36 percent win. Postelection fundraisers easily recouped the $3 million he had lent to his campaign.

Despite his margin of victory, Mike Foster took office knowing that many had voted for him primarily because he was white and he was not Edwin Edwards. He wanted to demonstrate that his administration would reach higher than the lowest common denominator.

No act made that point so clearly as when the governor-elect introduced his new commissioner of administration, PAR President Mark Drennen. As the best-known Cabinet member, Drennen brought a depth of credibility and good-government credentials to the new administration.

From legislative fiscal officer to PAR president, Drennen called himself "the luckiest person in the world . . . to take everything I had learned for twenty years and not say what we ought to do but now could go do it."

There was just one catch. He said that Foster told him, "You can talk about anything you want to talk about, except the homestead exemption."

Drennen called it "a good deal," though many PAR members and business leaders groaned in disappointment that the new business-oriented governor, a PAR member no less, would reject the centerpiece of tax reform. Foster had held a dim view of property taxes since the U.S. Supreme Court ruled that non–property owners had the right to vote in property tax elections. To drive the point home, he backed a bill to raise the exemption to $100,000. It would fail, but it also put the issue on ice for the rest of his first term.

Though heartened that the new administration was in good hands, PAR leaders had a vacancy to fill at the top. As with Drennen, they focused on research strength and a practical working knowledge of state government when they chose Jacklyn Ducote as the sixth president of PAR.

At the time, Ducote was LABI's executive vice-president in charge of coordinating research and policy development. Before that, she had been LABI's chief education staffer, a job Ed Steimel had lured her to from her thirteen-year career at PAR as researcher, librarian and public information director. Education reform was Ducote's passion, but she had firsthand experience, both at PAR and at LABI, in dealing with the major issues that had faced the state over the past 30 years.

As Ducote took the reins at PAR, one of those issues was coming to the fore. With the defeat of some senior lawmakers tainted by the federal gambling investigation, the new governor and new Legislature felt compelled to address public distrust of the ethics of public officials.

Fortunately, they had a timely blueprint to work from, the newly published recommendations from the joint ethics study by PAR and the Bureau of Governmental Research.

The PAR and BGR report laid the groundwork for the host of ethics reforms that would be passed in the 1996 special session, including creation of a single, strong ethics board; computerization of campaign finance records and access to them via the Internet; tightened lobbyist reporting requirements; the end to retirement benefits for legislators and other part-time public officials; and a ban on campaign contributions from gambling interests, a law later overturned by the state Supreme Court.

PAR gave the governor and Legislature high marks when it published an ethics scorecard, but it noted that several important recommendations were not considered. Among them were a ban on all state and local contracts with legislators; a prohibition on elected officials creating or controlling political action committees; annual personal financial disclosure reports from all elected and key appointed state and parish officials; and a $50,000 limit on the use of postelection fundraisers to repay a candidate's loans to his own campaign.

Yet there remained one area of choosing public servants that campaign finance reform alone could not address. In July 1996, PAR recommended that Louisiana follow the national trend toward merit selection of judges, at least at the appellate and Supreme Court levels. The report went against the grain of public opinion in a state that holds more elections for more offices than any other in the Union. That summer, Mike Foster would thrust himself into a state Supreme Court election when he labeled trial lawyers "the bad guys" and rallied the business sector to pump money into Chet Traylor's successful campaign to unseat Justice Joe Bleich.

The escalation in spending on judicial races indicates that, like lowering the homestead exemption, this PAR recommendation will not be fulfilled for some time.

Such reticence toward change on the part of politicians sharpened PAR's focus on empowering citizens in the public arena. In 1996, PAR reassessed the state's sunshine laws and updated the citizens' rights card, which has been credited with ensuring cooperation of public officials at all levels, especially locally.

As longtime supporters of public education, PAR and Jackie Ducote participated on the Foster-appointed LEARN Commission that led to emphasizing accountability both for educators, through a statewide grading system for schools, and for students, by requiring fourth- and eighth-graders to pass standardized tests before advancing to the next grade.

Yet Ducote had fought enough battles with the public education system to know that laws were not enough. In 1997, PAR updated the charter school handbook that Ducote had first published at LABI to help local organizers navigate the myriad requirements in the law. An independent evaluation of the fledgling charter school program cited the handbook as the single most helpful tool for organizers. Noted Ducote, "If people starting a school had to go find all that on their own, they would never get started."

As the Foster administration poured new resources into basic and higher education, the area in between, postsecondary adult education, presented a challenge for policymakers. For years, the vocational-technical schools had been the stepchildren of the Board of Elementary and Secondary Education as well as patronage fiefdoms for legislators. The new community colleges coming into existence were getting the same treatment.

Since one of its first reports in the early 1950s, PAR had championed the need for better vo-tech school management and more community colleges. Experience showed that new money spent on both types of schools would be wasted without strong, centralized management. PAR did not like what it saw in its 1997 report on community colleges. The expansion plan was proceeding piecemeal with no overall plan or objectives. The Legislature had authorized new campuses despite negative feasibility reports from the Board of Regents.

PAR recommended creating a single board for vo-tech schools and community colleges that would be under the Board of Regents, the premier board of higher education.

That was not the approach favored by the Foster administration, which proposed an independent board that would coordinate vo-tech activities with BESE and community college affairs with Regents. With PAR Senior Research Associate Ty Keller on the study commission, PAR stuck to its position that postsecondary education would be compromised unless its board was under the control and protection of the Board of Regents. In one of PAR's more pleasant surprises, shortly before the commission issued its final report, the administration abandoned its initial proposal and embraced PAR's. There was political resistance from legislators, education employees and BESE, but the combined community and technical college board plan was adopted by lawmakers and approved by voters in 1998.

The combination of a better economy, tighter management and less money siphoned off to debt service enabled the Foster administration to avoid the budget shortfalls that had plagued governors and limited their effectiveness since the oil bust began in 1982. That fiscal stability and Mike Foster's own political prowess helped to restore much of the enormous executive power that had been eroded through past budgetary confrontations with the Legislature.

Toward the end of Foster's first term, he was as popular and powerful as any governor PAR had dealt with in five decades. Though the two shared many values and goals, Foster's style and PAR's longstanding distrust of the power wielded by Louisiana's governors made it nearly inevitable that they would clash.

Their collision would occur on U.S. 90.

The highway priority system PAR helped to create had stood the test of time and politicians for 25 years. For the most part, governors and legislators had not interfered with planners in the Department of Transportation and Development, who used traffic counts, safety concerns and road conditions to determine which projects would be scheduled each year.

The DOTD parameters did not fit a massive project favored by a group of businessmen in the Lafayette area to upgrade U.S. 90 from Lafayette to New Orleans to interstate standard. Their immediate objective was the construction of overpasses at the busiest and most dangerous intersections between Lafayette and Franklin. Though they had obtained federal designation for the "I-49 South" corridor, they were not getting anywhere with DOTD engineers until they won over Governor Foster to their cause.

Confident from an attorney general's opinion that he was within the highway priority law, the governor insisted that DOTD begin building the rural overpasses before constructing an expressway through Lafayette, where traffic was more congested.

When DOTD Secretary Frank Denton abruptly tendered his resignation, it was speculated that the retired army general was quitting because of the governor's intercession on U.S. 90.

PAR researcher Ty Keller had already had a bad experience with the administration when he served on a commission studying the need to extend the so-called TIMED program for building four-lane highways. "We got snookered on the TIMED commission," he said when the administration did not include language in the bill to reevaluate and set priorities for unfinished projects.

With Denton's resignation over the U.S. 90 matter, Keller feared that politics was interjecting itself into highway planning again. So Keller wrote and PAR President Ducote approved a two-page *PAR Commentary* entitled "My Way or the Highway." It stated that Foster was manipulating the highway priority system with "political log-rolling and power plays to secure pet projects."

The governor did not respond publicly, but he later said that he told Keller, "I'm going to let your membership look at this, and they're the people that you basically have to deal with." But he added, "I didn't ask them to threaten PAR."

Yet some did, as some members of the I-49 Task Force who also belonged to PAR called to say they were dropping their membership. Soon letters began to appear in the *Baton Rouge Advocate* criticizing PAR's commentary as well as DOTD's resistance to the upgrade of U.S. 90.

Then Foster asked to meet with PAR's executive committee and Ducote to give his side of the controversy. "He did most of the talking," said one committee member. The governor wanted PAR to say its commentary was incorrect, which the officers refused to do, though some admitted that the tone was more personal and adversarial than necessary.

The matter seemed at rest until a few days later when Ducote announced she was retiring for "personal reasons." At this point, the dispute between PAR and the governor was very public, and it did not reflect well on either.

"I hope to heck she's not quitting over this," said Foster.

But she was. "Jackie is very upset about it," her old friend and former boss Ed Steimel told the *Advocate*. "If she does leave, I don't think anybody will have any doubt that it occurred because of this, because she is a very principled person."

PAR Chairman Morris Mintz told the press that PAR stood behind its commentary, though it "could have been worded a little less confrontationally."

That was enough of a crack in the armor for the *Advocate* to turn its focus from Foster to PAR and lament in an editorial: "PAR leaders have risked sacrificing the future of a good organization to salve the governor's feelings. . . . The circumstances are such that it leaves a cloud hanging over the organization."

Neither PAR nor Foster backed down from their positions on whether he improperly manipulated the highway priority system. The state soon began building overpasses along U.S. 90, but the controversy did alert legislators in other parts of the state to question the level of funding for the interstate upgrade project in coming budgets.

The episode prompted soul searching among PAR leaders about whether the organization was straying from its role as an independent research group conducting its work free of board interference. Yet board members point out that "My Way or the Highway" was a commentary, not a *PAR Analysis* or *PAR Guide* that undergoes extensive prepublication review by the staff and the executive committee. Had the commentary undergone a similar review process, said members, the published result may have been different. As for staff independence, earlier executive committees had frequently reined in Ed Steimel when he crossed the line from research to advocacy.

In the end, while PAR did not lose any members over the commentary, it was again faced with replacing its president. And the organization's problems ran deeper than executive turnover.

As strong on research and public credibility as were Mark Drennen and Jackie Ducote, they did not place the same emphasis on fundraising, and the organization's bottom line reflected that view. By 1994, PAR revenues were 20 percent below their peak of ten years before. Adjusted for inflation, PAR in the 1990s operated on 20 percent less income than in 1954 and half the level of 1974. Its 21 full-time positions in 1975 had shrunk to 6 in 1995. In 1995, PAR took in $581,000 in revenues and spent $621,000.

To be fair, Drennen and Ducote's task was harder than it had been for Ed Steimel or Art Thiel in the days before LABI rose to become a dominant force in lobbying, electioneering and fundraising.

As PAR searched for a new president in 1995, the leadership heard from members who said the group needed a shot in the arm as well. "The organization had been doing the same thing for 20 to 30 years and needed to get with it," said Morris Mintz. At that time, PAR underwent a strategic planning review and wrote a new plan and mission statement. "That kind of turned us, but it didn't move us," said Mintz.

To move it, PAR needed a president as strong on fundraising as on research. It needed a leader to help it meet the challenges of the new political landscape without sacrificing its reputation for sound and timely policy review.

Just as PAR's founders used the Bureau of Governmental Research as a working model, the latter-day leadership would turn to the New Orleans organization for its new president, Jim Brandt. The Colorado native and Tulane graduate in urban studies possessed a clear-eyed view of how public policy worked, and didn't work, within the realm of Louisiana politics. He had served in the administration of former New Orleans Mayor Dutch Morial and on the governmental relations staff of the 1984 World's Fair. He had taught graduate-level courses in grant development and public administration before starting his own business managing other organizations.

He knew what he was getting into. When he took over BGR in 1987, it was in worse financial condition than was PAR in 1999. In twelve years, he had developed new revenue sources other than dues and increased annual income from $100,000 to $600,000.

This time, the personnel changes within PAR did not stop at the staff level. The board of directors had grown to more than 100. Said one member, "We had a bunch who were set in their ways. They would say, 'We've been doing it this way for twenty years.'"

In 1999, PAR's board of directors began a long-overdue revision of the organization's bylaws. One of the changes made was to reduce the size of the board to 30–40 members and the executive committee to about ten, which enabled both groups to be more effective and responsive. It also adopted a broader mission statement that would have PAR focus on not just government research but a wider consideration of public policy, including economic development.

Brandt went right to work rebuilding PAR's finances. By early 2000, his quest for new revenue sources resulted in new grants for operating expenses and research projects. He began attracting sponsorships to underwrite events and some publications. Brandt estimates PAR's income will increase by $150,000 for the 2000–01 fiscal year. The organization has rebuilt its reserves and set up a small endowment fund.

PAR's financial position was not all that needed rebuilding. Citing the group's aging membership, Brandt commented, "We need to heighten our visibility and raise our profile." He started by revamping that PAR mainstay, the annual conference. "The annual meeting will have wider appeal to a wider membership rather than just to policy wonks," said Brandt. In 2000, he moved away from the 50-year tradition of organizing the conference around a single topic by presenting a range of well-known speakers, led by *Time* managing editor Walter Isaacson, a Louisiana native.

Instead of one conference held in Baton Rouge, PAR now plans to schedule other annual meetings in New Orleans and Shreveport.

To meet the demands of the rapidly changing Information Age, PAR began rethinking its publications in the early 1990s. Mark Drennen wrote letters to legislators as issues developed during a session. Jackie Ducote introduced the *PAR Commentary* as a rapid-response vehicle. In 1997, PAR entered cyberspace at www.par-la.org, where one can read all its publications and even download the "Citizens' Rights Card on Open Meetings and Public Records."

Brandt has begun publishing four-page *PAR Briefs* every month, with plans for more during legislative sessions. He says that PAR will continue longer, in-depth research pieces on big issues.

In December 1999, with the United States economy completing its record-setting eighth straight year of peacetime recovery and the Congressional Budget Office projecting $1.9 trillion in budget surpluses over the next ten years, presidential candidates and state legislatures debated how much taxes should be cut. The picture was not so rosy in Louisiana. Gov. Mike Foster sent out a request to organizations and individuals to suggest means of funding teacher pay raises to reach the southern average in the face of a $630 million shortfall in the 2000–01 budget.

After the administration's charmed first term, the dysfunctional state tax code displayed the price Louisiana must pay for being different. The first *PAR Brief* under Brandt in January 2000 laid out much the same budget picture as one of the very first studies by the group in 1951. Louisiana relied more than most states on sales taxes and less than others on property and personal income taxes. PAR showed that Louisiana ranked 7th in the nation in sales taxes, 47th in property taxes and 41st out of 41 states that levy sales taxes.

Responding to the governor, PAR took the contrarian view that simply raising teacher pay to the southern average, while laudable, could serve to neglect overall education funding, in which Louisiana also trails the regional average. It cautioned that "legislative micromanagement" of this type would diminish local control, reduce opportunities for incentive pay and encourage teacher unions to bypass local school boards and go directly to the Legislature in the future, especially as the southern average continues to rise.

PAR recommended increasing personal income taxes, though the governor initially ruled out raising the low rates that are fixed in the constitution. The organization also proposed that he reconsider his opposition to gradually lowering the homestead exemption, along with the industrial tax exemption, which would enable parish school boards to take on more of the responsibility for funding education.

Though during his campaign the governor promised a sweeping approach to broadening the tax structure, the prognosis for true tax reform is no better now than it was 50 years ago. In that time, PAR has been a participant if not protagonist in major state reforms, from campaign finance to home rule to education accountability to the highway priority system. Its persistent recommendations have led to vast improvements in fiscal policy, including a required balanced budget, debt limitation and the Revenue Estimating Conference.

Yet the holy grail of tax reform has remained beyond PAR's reach, as governors and legislators have refused to put major changes to a vote, either of themselves or of the people.

It remains the major piece of unfinished business, for the organization and the state, as PAR enters its second half century. For that, and other issues that will form its future agenda for change, PAR may need to create new approaches for presenting its message to a new generation of leaders and voters.

In some ways, PAR has been a victim of its own success. By the mid-1990s, the Legislature had empowered itself to do what it had once looked to PAR for. Not only was it staffed up for research, but it also acted on that research—and PAR recommendations—to make more fiscally responsible choices. PAR's very first recommendation, the Legislative Council, was followed by the Legislative Auditor, the Legislative Fiscal Office, the Senate Fiscal Office and the Revenue Estimating Conference.

The state's daily newspapers, once reliant on PAR for government research, are doing better jobs themselves of reporting public affairs, especially regarding the Legislature, and exploring deeper political and economic issues.

The public has greater access than ever to information, but a great gulf remains between having information and knowing what it means and what to do with it. So much has changed in Louisiana and in the world since 114 concerned citizens gathered for lunch at the Bentley Hotel in the spring of 1950. Yet many intrinsic factors remain the same, such as powerful governors, compliant legislators and the lack of effective checks and balances on them.

As much as ever, Louisiana needs an organization, such as PAR, of citizens empowered with information, dedicated to nonpartisan research and willing to call it as it sees it and to let the chips fall where they may.

Presidents/Chairmen of PAR

From its beginnings in 1950, PAR has been led by individuals accomplished in business and professional life but also dedicated to improving the state of government in Louisiana. In the early years, the leaders of PAR carried the title *president,* while the staff was led by an *executive director.* In the late 1970s, the titles were changed to *chairman* and *president,* respectively.

F. Hugh Coughlin, 1950–51. The man who built up CLECO from a string of icehouses spearheaded PAR's organizational effort and first membership drive.

R. D. Kellogg, 1952–53. The Monroe lumberman and real estate executive made the motion to start PAR at its first organizational meeting.

Eben Hardie, 1954–55. The first president from New Orleans knew the worst of Louisiana politics from his service as foreman of the federal grand jury that delivered indictments in the Louisiana Scandals of 1939–40.

Ed Taussig, 1956. The Lake Charles automobile dealer helped PAR pass its first test of independence when he gave the go-ahead for a PAR study on idle state funds that caused a group of banks to drop their membership.

Joe D. Smith, 1957. The publisher of the *Alexandria Daily Town Talk* who served a term as president of the American Newspaper Publishers Association. Gov. John McKeithen appointed Smith the first president of the Coordinating Council of Higher Education, the forerunner of the Board of Regents.

Parrish Fuller, 1958. The Oakdale lumberman, touted as a reform candidate for governor in 1948, often provided Huey and Earl Long with a sounding board on the views of the business community.

Felix Kurz, 1959. The Lafayette insurance executive was considered an intellectual light on the PAR research committee, which determined the issues to be studied.

Charles Keller, 1960. The construction company owner in New Orleans was a leading philanthropist along with his wife, the former Rosa Freeman.

Ventress Young, 1961. The Bogalusa paper-mill executive took on the state's education establishment in his unsuccessful effort to get the state to compare the quality of all public schools.

Paul Brown, 1962. The Shreveport bank president and oil company executive twice served as head of the state Civil Service Commission.

John Deming, 1963. The Alexandria physician and member of the Rapides Parish School Board was a champion of public schools during the state's difficult early desegregation years.

Henry Voorhies, 1964. The vice-president of Humble Oil Company, the forerunner of Exxon, managed its giant refinery in Baton Rouge. He was the first LSU graduate to head PAR.

R. L. Lowrey, 1965. The car dealer from Many was the first small businessman to head PAR.

Kenneth Shaffer, 1966, 1968. The New Orleanian was president of Chevron Oil and head of the Louisiana division of the Mid-Continent Oil & Gas Association. He advocated returning to the policy of two-year terms for PAR presidents.

Clifford Strauss, 1967. The Monroe liquor wholesaler headed PAR as relations with Gov. John McKeithen deteriorated. In a stormy two-hour meeting in the Governor's Mansion, he refused McKeithen's demand to see PAR reports before publication.

E. A. Courtney, 1969–70. The vice-president of a natural gas and land company defended public education at emotional public meetings during the peak of the desegregation turmoil.

Edward Stauss Jr., 1971–72. The vice-president of Freeport Minerals Co. in New Orleans gave Ed Steimel the go-ahead to serve as the federal special master for the landmark reapportionment of the Louisiana Legislature into single-member districts. Stauss also chaired the important research committee for many years.

John L. McInnis, 1973–74. The owner of McInnis Construction Co., a major North Louisiana contractor, McInnis was a staunch defender of staff independence at PAR.

Wallace Armstrong, 1975–76. While president of PAR, the Ethyl Refinery manager in Baton Rouge helped found the Louisiana Association of Business and Industry. He worked hard to maintain PAR's identity and its membership roles during the challenging transition period from Ed Steimel to Art Thiel.

Richard Knight, 1977–78. The Bogalusa lawyer led an initiative to broaden PAR's membership ranks and to develop sponsorships among agribusiness and forestry companies.

Norman Kinsey Jr., 1979–80. The Shreveport oil and real estate investor started his presidency defending PAR's recommendation for local personnel systems in the face of strong criticism from the Louisiana Civil Service League.

L. H. Hebert Jr., 1981–82. The Thibodaux bank president supported Art Thiel in his criticism of the reform shortcomings of the business-friendly Treen administration.

Wiley Sharp, 1983–85. The Hammond businessman known for his wit served during the transition from Dave Treen to Edwin Edwards' third term as Louisiana slid into recession.

LeDoux Provosty Jr., 1985–87. The Alexandria attorney was the first second-generation PAR leader: his father was a founder and an original board member.

Bill Senn, 1987–89. The manager of Exxon Chemical was chairman during PAR's effort to achieve fiscal reform under Gov. Buddy Roemer.

Harry McCall Jr., 1989–91. The partner in the Chaffe McCall law firm in New Orleans and former King of Rex served for ten years on the state Board of Ethics for Elected Officials.

Charles Ellis Brown, 1991–93. The president of the Bayou State Oil Corporation in Shreveport was the son of 1962 PAR Chairman Paul Brown and father-in-law of 1996 PAR Chairman James Richardson.

Tommy James, 1993–95. The retired president of T. L. James & Co., a major Louisiana contractor, James was the first chairman of the Board of Regents, on which he served for 18 years.

James Richardson, 1995–97. The LSU economics professor has been a leading proponent of fiscal reform and serves as a member of the state Revenue Estimating Conference, which sets the amount of money that the Legislature may appropriate each year.

Morris Mintz, 1997–99. The president of a liquor wholesaling company in Monroe and grandson of former PAR chairman Clifford Strauss, Mintz helped PAR redefine its strategic mission.

Jay Handelman, 1999–2000. The public relations consultant with Freeport-McMoRan led PAR through the transition from Jackie Ducote to Jim Brandt.

Other PAR Publications

Your Louisiana Government: An Owner's Manual
Louisiana Charter School Handbook
Guide to the Proposed Constitutional Amendments
"Citizens' Rights Card on Open Meetings and Public Records Laws"
State Budget Analysis
Legislative Session Wrap-up
Legislative Bulletins
Research Briefs
PAR Quarterly Newsletter

For pricing and ordering information, call PAR at (225) 926-8414 or write P.O. Box 14776, Baton Rouge, LA 70898-4776.

THE PUBLIC AFFAIRS RESEARCH COUNCIL OF LOUISIANA

PAR is an independent voice, offering solutions to critical public issues in Louisiana through accurate, objective research and by focusing public attention on those issues.

As a private, nonprofit research organization, PAR is supported through the tax-deductible membership contributions of hundreds of Louisiana citizens who want better, more efficient and more responsive government.

Although PAR does not lobby, PAR's research gets results. Many significant governmental reforms can be traced back to PAR recommendations. Through its extensive research and public information program, PAR places constructive ideas and solutions into the mainstream of political thinking.

In addition to being a catalyst for governmental reform, PAR also has an extensive program of citizen education and serves as a watchdog on state government. The organization's 50 years of research on state and local government in Louisiana give it a unique historical perspective as well as the ability to monitor implementation of reforms and to remind public officials of promises made.

Membership in PAR is open to the public. For more information, contact PAR at (225) 926-8414 or write P.O. Box 14776, Baton Rouge, LA 70898-4776.

*Visit PAR's Website @
www.la-par.org.*

Other books by John Maginnis

THE LAST HAYRIDE
A colorful campaign chronicle of Edwin Edwards' 1983 election for governor.

CROSS TO BEAR
The Race from Hell between Edwin Edwards, David Duke and Buddy Roemer in 1991.

For direct orders, contact:

Darkhorse Press
P.O. Box 6
Baton Rouge, Louisiana 70821
1-800-673-5577